EXPOSITORY
STUDIES IN
GENESIS 2 and 3

A
DISCOVERY
BIBLE STUDY
BOOK

EXPOSITORY STUDIES IN GENESIS 2 and 3

UNDERSTANDING MAN

RAY C. STEDMAN

WORD BOOKS
PUBLISHER
4800 WEST WACO DRIVE
WACO, TEXAS
76703

EXPOSITORY STUDIES IN GENESIS 2 AND 3: *Understanding Man*

Discovery Books are published by Word Books, Publishers in cooperation with Discovery Foundation, Palo Alto, California.

ISBN 0-87680-984-0

Library of Congress catalog card number: 75-18257

Printed in the United States of America

First Printing, September 1975
Second Printing, April 1976
Third Printing, May 1976
Fourth Printing, September 1981

Contents

Preface

In this brief study on *Understanding Man*, I have attempted to bring into focus some of the principles of true psychology and true anthropology. It is by these biblical principles that all secular studies ultimately must be measured, for here is the revelation of things as they really are with respect to mankind.

Our task is to find clues to unravel the greatest mystery ever written—the story of man. We are seeking to understand ourselves, both as men and women "in Adam" and also as the new men and women we have become if we are "in Christ." But we must begin with the first Adam because what he was, we are.

It always strikes me as strange that anyone can deny the reality of the story of the Fall of man, especially when the very man who denies it is himself repeating it, perhaps dozens of times a day. Temptation follows the same pattern with us that it did with Eve in the garden of Eden, and the process is absolutely relentless.

We may think, sometimes, that our guilt is hidden from the eyes of men, since no one else knows about it, and nothing has come down on us. Yet within us, whenever we yield to evil, a darkness falls and death tightens its grip upon our throat.

Here, then, is a study aimed at first, understanding the unchanging process of temptation in our lives, and then, at unfolding the unchanging process of God's grace which seeks us out and restores us.

But the grace of God often goes unrecognized for what it is. In this passage of Genesis, if we understand it properly, God has revealed more clearly than perhaps anywhere else in the Bible how unwilling he is that any should perish. Far from merely pronouncing judgment on Adam and Eve, he gives them an assurance of life beyond the death of their bodies, and a clear promise of a Redeemer to come.

I hope your heart will be lifted with fresh encouragement as mine has been, when you discover the loving purpose behind God's expulsion of the first man and woman from the garden. On that purpose hangs the whole truth of the gospel of Christ.

RAY C. STEDMAN

1 / Was Adam for Real?

I was sitting in the airport of Guatemala City, working on the early stages of this book, and I faced a large
mural, depicting life among the ancient Mayan Indians.
As I sat in that fascinating country, under the shadow
of great volcanoes which had been rumbling and muttering all afternoon, and thought of the history of the
Mayans—that strange race we know so little about—I
felt anew the mystery of history. Civilizations have risen
and flourished for centuries and then in a strange way,
often for unknown reasons, have died and are now buried
in humid jungles, forgotten fragments of ancient history. The question came to me again as it comes to
any who think about the past, where did this human
race begin? How did these strange beings come into
existence? For what purpose?

These are questions that have forever fascinated men.
To my knowledge there is only one book that gives us
a reliable answer to these questions. Scientists, of course,
are trying to discover facts from the ancient past, but
even they admit that their efforts are but a kind of feeling around in the dark after a few fragments. But this
book of God, bearing upon it the seal of authority of

the Lord Jesus Christ, has revealed to us all man needs to know to solve the riddle of life. I wish I could impress upon young and old alike the truth of that statement. Here is all we need to know about humanity, revealed in the pages of Scripture, especially designed that we might know the facts about life.

It is no slight exaggeration to say that there are no writings more important for the proper understanding of history and man than the first chapters of Genesis. Here is hidden the secret of man's sinfulness, that terrible mystery of evil and darkness which continually confronts us in this modern world. In this section is the key to the relationship of the sexes, the proper place of man and woman in marriage, the solution to the problem of mounting divorce rates, and other marital issues that abound in modern society.

Here, also, is the explanation for the struggle of life, and here great light is thrown on the problems of work and leisure. In these chapters is the first and fundamental revelation of the meaning of divine redemption and grace, and here the essential groundwork is laid for the understanding of the cross of Jesus Christ. This whole section is unprecedented in its importance.

But because it is so important, it has been heavily attacked. These two chapters have often been rejected outright as simply repugnant to modern man. There are cults which reject them as being utterly inconsistent with what man wants to believe about himself. Sometimes the chapters have been dismissed with contempt as merely a collection of ancient myths or legends with no significance for modern minds.

And sometimes they have been treated as containing important truths, but needing to be (in the favorite word of many today in theological circles) "demytholo-gized." To quote one of the writers of this school:

> There is truth of great vitality and power in many passages of which the strictly historical accuracy may be questioned. It is our job therefore to find the truth that may be buried under some layers of legend.

Before I discuss the meaning and intense significance of these passages with you I must first dispose of these objections. Many are bothered by these problems, and lest we seem to ignore them, I want to deal with them to some extent now, and in subsequent chapters we will come to the actual meaning of the passage.

The Documentary Theory

There are two general lines of attack upon the story of Adam and Eve in the garden of Eden. One is an attempt to destroy the literary integrity of the text; the other attempts to deny the historical accuracy of these accounts. The first approach is based upon the claim that this section of Genesis (and probably the whole of the first five books of the Bible) were not written by Moses, as the Bible claims, but that they were actually composed by an unknown editor (whom these scholars call a redactor) who lived long after David and Solomon, and who may have lived even as late as the Babylonian captivity, only some 500 years before Christ.

The critics claim that the redactor was not writing down things that were revealed to him by any divine process, but was only recording certain tales of the women who gathered around the wells and talked over various legends of their past. They claim he collected the tales of travelers and others, and thus recorded for posterity these early legends of man.

The support for this idea arises out of certain changes of style in this passage, and the use of the divine name in a different form. You will notice that in chapter two, verse four the name, "the Lord God" appears for the first time. Previously in Genesis there has only been the name, "God," which is a translation of the Hebrew, "Elohim." But here we have the Lord God, or in Hebrew, Jehovah Elohim, and all through this section that name is used. It has been suggested therefore that you can identify the various stories, and the changes in authorship, by the use of the divine names.

Now, fully developed, this has evolved into what is called today, "the documentary theory of Genesis." Some unknown editor has collected from various sources these documents which can be identified by certain marks within them, and has put them all together, using excerpts from here, and excerpts from there, and blending them together into the books that we now know as Genesis, Exodus, Leviticus, Numbers, and Deuteronomy—the Pentateuch, the five books of Moses.

This whole idea has been supported by certain piece-meal evidence taken from the Scriptures. Scholars have gone through the books and extracted certain ideas of passages that seemed to support their theory, but ignoring others that would contradict it. This documentary theory gained wide support, but has long ago been fully answered by both Jewish and Christian writers. Remarkably enough, it still persists, even though it is increasingly difficult to hold.

Forty years ago, Dr. Lyman Abbott spoke at the University of California at Berkeley. He was, at that time, a noted liberal scholar working on the origin of scriptural books. He said something like this, "Young gentlemen, I feel that perhaps I am as qualified as anyone to speak in this field of the origins of the books of the Bible, and I want to warn you against going too far in basing your conclusions upon the so-called 'assured results of modern scholarship.' As one of these modern scholars, I know that these results are not always as 'assured' as they seem to be. My careful conclusion is that the first five books of the Bible were either written by Moses—or by someone else named Moses!" Perhaps that is about as far as we need to go in laying to rest the documentary theory of the Scriptures.

No Talking Serpent

Now the second attack upon this section is more frequently pressed today. This is the idea that there are great truths about man here—his fears, his evil, his hungers are all set forth in a remarkable way and we can learn much about ourselves—but these truths are conveyed deliberately to us in the language of myth. Perhaps Moses did write this, they say, or some other unknown writers. But at any rate, the authors were attempting to convey to us mighty truths through the language of myth, adopting a kind of parabolic vehicle in order to convey these truths to us. There was, of course, no literal tree in a literal garden; there were no actual beings named Adam and Eve; and, of course, there was no talking serpent or forbidden fruit.

It is all somewhat like the myth of Santa Claus. Everyone today (except Virginia) knows that there is no real Santa Claus, but the idea behind Santa Claus—cheerful jollity, a reward for good behavior, and a universal kindness of spirit—are all true. If we forget the myth of Santa Claus we still have left a core of truth which is conveyed to us by the story of Santa Claus. Thus we can treat these opening chapters of Genesis much in the same way. You can take the story of Adam and Eve, they say, and throw away the form by which it is conveyed and you will still have a germ of truth about the human race.

But have you? What do we say to this kind of approach? We must say that we reject the whole approach as biblically untenable, scientifically unsound, and, in the end, totally destructive of truth and faith. Let me give the reasons for this.

First of all, this approach violates the integrity of the Book of Genesis. Where does myth end and history begin? Where is the line of demarcation? If Adam and Eve are a myth, then so is the story of Cain and Abel. And if Cain and Abel are a myth, then so are Noah and the flood. Since the record moves right on without a break into the story of Abraham, Isaac, and Jacob, are we to assume that these, too, are myths? If so, where does history begin? How can you detect the place where myth, fantasy, and legend end, and actual human history begins?

If we examine the first chapter of Genesis (which is likewise termed myth) we can see that it is not a myth at all. It is in accord with the true discoveries of modern science and, in fact, anticipates and corrects much of modern science. When you begin looking for myths in these Old Testament stories, you will find that it is impossible to draw the line anywhere except where you, for some emotional reason, may choose to draw it.

Such a process carries right over into the New Testament and the story of the virgin birth becomes a myth, and even the story of the incarnation itself. The Christmas story becomes nothing but a beautiful parable, designed to express truth, but not true in history. Also the stories of the miracles of Jesus and the resurrection and the crucifixion . . . where do you stop?

Well, the answer is that you do not stop. All these stories have actually been termed myth, which supports my contention that there is no stopping place when you apply this kind of a theory to the biblical records. Of course, if you treat the Bible that way, then you must in all good conscience treat any other ancient document in the same way. If you carry this out to its logical conclusion we are left without any knowledge whatsoever of the ancient world, nothing that we can trust. The theory destroys too much to be acceptable.

There *is* myth in the Scripture. There are legends which are reported to us in various places in the Bible. But the significant thing is that they are identified as such. You can find them in both the Old and New Testaments, but the writers of the Scripture were aware of their nature as myths and recorded them as such.

Furthermore, there are passages throughout both the Old and New Testaments which warn against believing in myths or taking them seriously. Peter warns against this, saying that the stories he and the other apostles told were not cleverly designed myths, but were actual historic occurrences (2 Pet. 1:16). Paul writes to his son in the faith, Timothy, and warns him against being influenced by godless myths and old wives' fables (1

Tim. 4:7). The apostles were aware of this kind of danger to faith and warned against it even in the early days of our Christianity.

Second, this approach of myth contradicts the usage of the Lord Jesus Christ and of the apostles themselves. If you believe that the story of Adam and Eve is a myth then you immediately find yourself clashing with the authority of the Lord Jesus Christ. In Matthew it is recorded that our Lord, facing the questions of the Pharisees about divorce, said, "He who made them from the beginning made them male and female" (Matt. 19:4). If you accept that as a statement from One who declared himself to be the truth and who told only the truth, then you must accept this story of Adam and Eve as factual.

Beginning with Moses

The Lord Jesus constantly referred to Moses as the author of the Pentateuch and said, again and again, that what Moses wrote he, himself, fulfilled. In that wonderful scene in Luke, he walks with two men along the Emmaus road after the resurrection, and they do not recognize him. He asks them why they are so downcast and sorrowful, and they tell him of the strange events that have been occurring in Jerusalem, how one was crucified, a Jesus of Nazareth. Then we are told, "beginning with Moses and all the prophets, he interpreted to them in all the scriptures the things concerning himself" (Luke 24:27). Later on he appeared to them and rebuked them because they had not believed Moses and the prophets in the things written about him.

Never once did our Lord suggest that anything in the Old Testament was to be questioned as to its historical veracity. He refers to most of the miracles that are the source of problems to critics today, and speaks of them in such a way as to confirm and attest the fact that they were historical events, including Jonah and the fish and other stories.

Remember also that the Apostle Paul reminded Timothy that Adam was made first, and then Eve, just as the story in Genesis tells us. He says further that Adam was not deceived, but Eve was, and thus Adam went into sin deliberately, but Eve was blinded (1 Tim. 2: 13,14).

In Paul's second letter to the Corinthians, he refers to the serpent and is afraid that as the serpent deceived Eve, so the thoughts of his readers would be led astray by Satan's cunning (2 Cor. 11:3). In Romans and First Corinthians he compares Adam and Jesus, and indicates they are both individual men, the heads of two separate races. "As sin came into the world through one man," he said, [by *one* man], ". . . and spread to all men," so by one man redemption came (Rom. 5:12). If Jesus was an individual, then Adam was an individual, too. Again in Corinthians he draws a comparison between these two, pointing out that we were all born in Adam, and if we are born again, we are all in Christ (1 Cor. 15: 45). He puts the two on an individual basis. Therefore, if we approach these early chapters of Genesis with the idea that these are myths, legends, not really historical events, we are thus holding that the Apostle Paul knew less than we know about such matters.

Third, the whole idea of myth is ultimately destructive of the teaching of Scripture, of biblical theology. Why do men invent these suggestions of myth? If you investigate their reasons (though they may seldom admit this) it is obviously because they want to square these stories of Adam and Eve with the teachings of evolution. They do not want to admit that there was a couple named Adam and Eve that began the human race, but that there were, rather, a group of hominids who ascended from the animal kingdom and became men. In accordance with the theory of evolution you cannot trace humanity back to only a single couple.

But if evolution as the explanation of man's origin is true, then there never was a fall of man. Either man was created perfect—body, soul, and spirit—as Genesis tells us, or he has been slowly developing from the animal kingdom, and was never perfect. It is either one or the other. Either man fell from perfection or he was never perfect. And if he never has been perfect, then what is the point of redemption? If all we are doing is moving toward an ultimate goal of perfection, then what was the value of the work of Christ upon the cross?

You see, certain fundamental issues come in immediately, certain fundamental questions arise: Do we really need salvation? Are we not moving steadily toward a goal which will ultimately be reached, whether Christ died or not? What is the purpose, therefore, of his redeeming grace? The minute you interject mythical ideas into the opening chapters of Genesis you come into an immediate clash with the doctrine of atonement and of the redemption of man.

Demolished Claims

Finally, this mythical interpretation denies the scientific evidence which does exist to support the historical truths of these events. It has been almost humorous, during the last forty or fifty years, the many, many times the pompous claims of the "higher critics" have been completely demolished by the archaeologist's spade. Again and again evidence has been turned up to prove that what the Bible says is true and what the critics claim has been false. In fact, there has not been one instance of the reverse, in which a biblical event has been proved to be false by archaeology—not one—but scores of instances where the Bible has been substantiated.

There is, for instance, considerable archaeological evidence that Nimrod, who is mentioned in the fourth chapter of Genesis, existed as a historical person. Further, Lamech and Zillah, his wife, and Tubalcain, their son, are supported as historical characters by archaeology. In fact, their names have passed into the language, describing some of the activities in which they were engaged. In the fourth chapter of Genesis there is a statement that Cain (this is the son of Adam, remember) went out and built a city and called the name of the city after his son, Enoch.

Interestingly enough, in the ancient cuneiform writings there is reference to a city named Unuk, which is clearly related to this name, Enoch, and it is called simply, "the city." Further, this name Enoch later passed into the language as the word for city. Through a process of philological transliteration (with which any linguist is familiar), this was changed from Enoch to "wark," and later to the word "perg," and then to the word "burgh," and it is still present in our language today in that form, as in Pitts*burgh*.

It is not unscientific to believe that Adam and Eve were actual, individual human beings; that Cain and Abel were likewise historical personages; that there was a Garden of Eden, and a tree in the midst of it. There is nothing unscientific about these stories and no scientific evidence in any way gainsays them. Any claim of this sort is simply an attack upon this record to try to destroy the historical accuracy of these accounts, and thus to undermine the great and central teaching of the Scriptures concerning the redemption of man.

When you get through analyzing this you stand where Christians have always stood, face to face with a choice: whether to accept the subjectivity of human wisdom, or the authority of the Son of God. It is one or the other. Was Jesus right, or were the critics right? It is either Christ or the critics. It has always been and always will be.

I, for one, do not think there is any reason to even debate the matter. I believe the Lord Jesus Christ stands as authority in every realm in which he speaks. When we consider the extent and nature of his authority, his knowledge of the world in which we live and of the human race and the mind of man; and contrast these with the puny, finite knowledge of struggling, sinful, human beings who see through a glass darkly, and who understand little of what they see, I find there is no real comparison at all.

This is why we must take these passages literally as they are, and treat them as historic accounts which are given to us to open to our understanding the problems we are facing daily. When we do, we discover they unfold to us great and marvelous truths that help us to grasp and understand life, and to rise in victory over the problems that beset us, and the forces that oppose us.

May I therefore urge you, in reading these passages, to do as the Lord Jesus reminded us, to take the place of a little child who is simply listening, carefully, quietly, to what he is told, thoughtfully investigating these things, and not questioning whether they are right or wrong, whether they are historical or unhistorical. There are no minds capable of establishing that today and there is no evidence capable of disproving it. If we settle that, we can come to these accounts, read them carefully through, and open our minds to the teaching of the Holy Spirit so that we might grasp these great and hidden things, remembering that as we come to know the truth about ourselves and the world in which we live, that truth will increasingly set us free.

We thank you, our Holy Father, for these stories. We pray for a childlike mind which will trust and believe and always be ready to be instructed; for an open, responsive heart, ready to obey as truth becomes apparent and applicable to our situation. We thank you for the One who has come to speak the truth, who declared himself to be the truth. What a great foundation our faith rests upon in this Holy One. In his name we pray, Amen.

2 / The Making of Man

Between chapter one of Genesis and chapter two, there is an obvious change of atmosphere. Genesis one is a very simple narrative of the creation of the world; the heavens and the earth, the plants and animals, and finally man. Simple, yet it is majestic in its beauty and profound in its depth. But when we come to chapter two we find a kind of recapitulation of the main event of chapter one, the creation of man. Here we are given in much greater detail the story of God's making of man.

Here also we are focusing upon other ideas that are introduced in the biblical text for the first time. For instance, as I have mentioned already, the name of God appears in a different form here. For the first time we have the great name of God that appears in so much of the rest of the Bible, Jehovah Elohim (or in the Hebrew, *Yahweh*), translated in our version, the "Lord God." There is a special reason for this change. Chapter one deals with the making of things, and God is presented to us under the name of Elohim, the Creator. But when man appears on the scene, God is referred to by the title of Jehovah, which means essentially the covenant-making God, the God who keeps a promise. It is particularly significant that when God first reveals himself to this race of ours, it is as a God who intends to keep his promises.

In chapter two there are several fascinating references in a number of fields of human thought. But the supreme aim of the chapter is unquestionably theological. It is the desire of the writer here to bring us to the tree of the knowledge of good and evil in the garden of Eden, and thus to the testing of man. That is one of the most important revelations we have about our fallen race. But let us begin with a chronological note:

> These are the generations of the heavens and the earth when they were created. In the day that the Lord God made the earth and the heavens, when no plant of the field was yet in the earth and no herb of the field had yet sprung up—for the Lord God had not caused it to rain upon the earth, and there was no man to till the ground; but a mist went up from the earth and watered the whole face of the ground—*then* the Lord God formed man . . . (Gen. 2:4–7).

You will notice the emphasis here upon the little time word, "then." Undoubtedly this rendering of the Revised Standard Version is the most accurate translation of the Hebrew. It is somewhat different from the King James text, and may even create more problems, but it is certainly more true to the original. The amazing thing is that here we have the creation of man linked to the *third* day of creation when the land emerged from the seas, and plant life began to appear.

The third and sixth days of creation link together in a most unusual way. This present text lends credence to the theory of a recapitulation: days one, two, and three; then, in a strange and rather remarkable way which no one fully understands, days four, five, and six are linked with the first three days (days one and four, two and five, three and six). I point this out for your own intellectual challenge, to open your mind to the possibility of viewing these accounts of creation in a different light from the conventional six-day approach.

It is also obvious that different conditions prevailed on earth in those early days than prevail now. There was no rain upon the earth, but a mist watered the ground. It is possible that this condition continued until the flood; it may be as some have suggested, that the rain that fell during the days of the flood were the first rains to occur upon earth, though geology would suggest otherwise. At least it is clearly apparent that conditions were greatly different in the distant past.

Man Out of Dust

Now we come to a most remarkable unfolding of the make-up of man:

> . . . then the Lord God formed man of dust from the ground, and breathed into his nostrils the breath of life; and man became a living being [or literally, a living soul] (Gen. 2:7).

Here is a condensed account of some tremendously significant things. We do not need to quibble over just how God formed the body of man. Did he pile dirt together, wet it with water to make a mud-statue, and then breathe life into it? No one knows. Certainly when we consider the miracle of conception and birth, when two tiny, almost invisible, cells meet together and begin to grow and divide under a rigid interlock of controls, developing at last into a human being such as we see ourselves to be, we need not ask about the ability of God to make man in his own remarkable way. Perhaps the event occurred along the line of the development of birth. We need not be concerned about the questions which people in the past have beat each other over the head with. Whether Adam had a navel or not is of little significance to me. What we are told here is that there are three divisions in man.

God first made the body of man, forming it from the dust of the earth. It is true that the same elements that are found in the dust of the ground are found also in the body of man. It is to dust that we return. You may recall the story of the little boy who came in to his mother and said excitedly, "Mother, is it true that we are made from the dust and that after we die we go back to the dust?" She said, "Yes, it is." "Well," he said, "I looked under my bed this morning, and there's someone either coming or going!"

We may not fully understand all that is involved in these pregnant sentences of Genesis 2:7, but it is important to notice that though the body of man was evidently formed first, yet the text itself does not say, "the body" but it says God formed *man* of dust from the earth. That has significance. Man is more than a body. He is not merely an animated piece of beefsteak, a hunk of meat with a nervous system. He is more than body; he is soul as well. The functions of the soul are wonderfully linked to those of the body in ways that we have not even begun to fathom.

For instance, the functions of the soul (reason, emotion, and will) are also in a remarkable way functions of our physical life. Reason is related to the brain, for it is only as the brain operates that reason occurs. Glands have great power over our emotional life. The hormones which they secrete directly affect us emotionally. Thus the functions of the soul are tied most remarkably to the body, and no one fully understands the mystery of it. In forming man, God made body and soul together, with the capacities for the function of the soul lying dormant within the body of man.

Breath of Life

Then, into this body with an inactive soul, the account says God breathed, through the nostrils, a living spirit. The phrase, breath of life, in the Hebrew, means a *spirit* of life. The words for breath and spirit are the same, both in Hebrew and in Greek, so that this is more than simply a picture of God breathing into man's nostrils. This is not face-to-face resuscitation; it is the impartation of a spirit into man. As we know from other Scripture passages, the spirit is our essential nature. It is this that distinguished man so remarkably from the animal creation. Thus as man comes into being, he comes full-orbed, as a threefold being, existing in body, soul, and spirit.

It is the joining together of spirit and body which activates and galvanizes the soul, so that it begins to function. Perhaps you can see something of the same principle in the operation of an electric light bulb. By itself a bulb is simply some wire and glass, rather commonplace, but with a remarkable potential. Add an invisible substance, electricity, and pass it through that visible wire, and a third function is born: light. Light is different from the wire, and different from the electricity, but comes streaming forth from that bulb. It is very much the same way with man. God made a body, with its possibilities of function as a soul, and breathed into it a spirit, and the union of body and spirit produced the activity of soul, as light is produced from the wire and electricity.

When the spirit passes from the body, the life of the body ends. James tell us, "the body apart from the spirit is dead" (Jas. 2:26). We bury the body, and the spirit returns to God who made it, the Scriptures say. Whatever portion of the soul (or the life of man—that part of us that has functioned within this time and space continuum) which has been saved, also returns with the spirit to God. I think it is significant to note that in the Scriptures, the spirit is regenerated but the soul is saved. There is only one place to my recollection, in which Scripture ever mentions a spirit being saved. It is the soul, the life that we are living now, that needs to be saved. That part of it which is lived in the power of the Spirit of God, functioning in relationship to the Lord Jesus Christ as God intended man to live, is saved. Our souls are thus *being* saved as we live day by day in relationship to the son of God. That "saved" soul is what we have left after this life, and only that. All else is wood, hay, and stubble, to disappear in the judging flame of God.

Now in fallen man, the spirit that is given to man is dead. This is what the Scripture means when it says man is dead in trespasses and sin. His spirit does not function as it should. Therefore the soul, which reflects like a mirror the activities of the spirit, reflects a lifeless nature. This is what creates the intense, worldwide restlessness of our race, the inability to be satisfied, the unending search for answers that are never found. It is all an expression of a wasted spirit, lying ruined within us because of the fall of man. But in the beginning as Adam came perfect from the hand of God, he was a lamp— and a lamp that was lit; alive in ways beyond anything that we can conjecture.

Now the third note of this passage is geographical:

> And the Lord God planted a garden in Eden, in the east; and there he put the man whom he had formed. And out of the ground the Lord God made to grow every tree that is pleasant to the sight and good for food, the tree of life also in the midst of the garden, and the tree of the knowledge of good and evil.
>
> A river flowed out of Eden to water the garden, and there it divided and became four rivers. The name of the first is Pishon; it is the one which flows around the whole land of Havilah, where there is gold; and the gold of that land is good; bdellium and onyx stone are there. The name of the second river is Gihon; it is the one which flows around the whole land of Cush. And the name of the third river is Tigris [or Hiddedel] which flows east of Assyria. And the fourth river is the Euphrates (Gen. 2: 8–14).

Here is the account of man placed in a garden. In passing I might point out that the name of the garden is never given to us. The name of it was not Eden; it was a garden placed in the land of Eden. The region in which the garden was found is called Eden, but the name of the garden itself is not given. There is no suggestion here that the whole earth was a garden, as we sometimes mistakenly conjecture. God marked off a certain division of it which he turned into a garden, and there he placed man. The task of man in that garden was to learn there the secrets that would enable him to turn the rest of the earth into a garden. But because man failed in the garden, he was unable to discover those secrets and, instead of turning the world into a garden, he is turning it into a garbage dump.

The proof that this account is no myth is that two of the rivers mentioned can still be identified. We have certain geographical landmarks given to us. Remember that this account describes a place that existed before the flood had undoubtedly widely changed the surface of the earth. Yet, certain of these rivers can be identified. The Tigris and the Euphrates, of course, still bear those names. The other two rivers are perhaps identical with certain streams which still flow, one into the Black Sea and the other into the Caspian Sea, both arising out of the mountains of Ararat in Armenia, where the ark rested after the flood.

There is an interesting reference here to the gold of the land. If you are familiar with Greek mythology, you know that the story of Jason and the Golden Fleece is set in this same area. It was to this part of the earth that Jason went in his search for the Golden Fleece. Thus the idea of gold has been associated with this land for a long time. The account is not myth but it is grounded in history, as is all of Scripture. These accounts are indeed symbolical, but they have roots solidly grounded in history.

Now the final and most important note is theological:

> The Lord God took the man and put him in the garden of Eden to till it and keep it. And the Lord God commanded the man, saying,

> "You may freely eat of every tree of the garden; but of the tree of the knowledge of good and evil you shall not eat, for in the day that you eat of it you shall die" (Gen. 2:15–17).

We must now take a look at these trees in the midst of the garden and their fruit. Once it was the fashion to deride this whole account as being ridiculous. The idea of Adam and Eve partaking of an actual fruit that had an evil effect upon them has been ridiculed and derided for many years. Yet, in these days of increased drug abuse we should hardly expect such disdain to be exhibited any longer. Now we well know that there are drugs and chemical agents present in fruits and other plants that can have this effect upon man. We know that many of these drugs have a most powerful effect, not only upon the human mind, stimulating it in strange, mysterious, and even dangerous ways, but we know also that they can affect even the chromosome structure of the body and pass along defects to children yet unborn. This is exactly the story of the garden of Eden.

Just as today we see young people drawn by the lure and attractiveness of psychedelic experiences, so Eve was drawn to this strange and mysterious fruit that hung before her, luring her powerfully with promises of strange and wonderful things that would satisfy and fulfill her, but which, in the actual partaking, would injure and damage and destroy the whole race that would follow. We need struggle no longer with the literalness of this account.

It is interesting that after this brief appearance in Genesis, the tree of the knowledge of good and evil disappears from Scripture, primarily because its effects have become commonplace. But the tree of life does convey immortality to man, and as such is used in Scripture as a symbol of the Lord Jesus Christ. In the Book of Revelation the tree of life appears as a symbol of the person of Christ. Paul wrote to Timothy and said of Christ that he "abolished death and brought life and immortality to light through the gospel" (2 Tim. 1:10). As we come to the Lord Jesus Christ and are related to him, we experience that which was the capability of this tree of life in the garden of Eden, from which man was ultimately excluded.

What is This Tree?

But what is this tree of the knowledge of good and evil? That is the question that looms before us as we look at this chapter. After all, what is wrong with knowing good and evil? Surely it is a good thing to know the difference between good and evil. Many Scripture passages encourage us to become mature enough to be able to distinguish between good and evil, and one mark of immaturity in a Christian is that he cannot tell the difference. He is like a child, like a worldling; he does not know how to distinguish between good and evil. But if it is a good thing to know the difference between good and evil why did God forbid Adam to partake of this fruit?

We get a little more light if we look ahead to chapter three where, in the story of the fall of man, we have the words of the serpent to the woman. He said to her,

> "For God knows that when you eat of it
> your eyes will be opened, and you will be like
> God, knowing good and evil" (Gen. 3:5).

Now everything the Devil says is not a lie. He uses truth, or rather, misuses truth in order to draw us on until we become the victims, ultimately, of his lie. But he baits his trap with truth, and here is the truth from the lips of the Devil. "You will," he says, "have your eyes opened when you eat of this fruit, and you will be like God, knowing good and evil." That suggests a clue as to what this fruit was and what it did.

How does God know good and evil? Think about it for a moment and you will see that God knows evil, not by experience because he cannot experience evil, but by relating it to himself. That which is consistent with his character and his nature is good; that which is inconsistent with it is evil. That which is out of line, out of character with himself is evil, destructive, and dangerous; but all that is in line with his own nature is good. That is how God "knows" good and evil. He relates it to himself.

It Was All a Lie

But God is the only one who can properly do that. God is the only Being in all the universe who has the right to relate all things to himself. When a creature tries it he gets into trouble. The creatures of God's universe are made to discover the difference between good and evil by relating all to the Being of God, not to themselves. When man ate of the fruit he began to do what God does—to relate everything to himself. Yet, as a creature, he has no real ability to maintain this kind of relationship and thus he is constantly interjecting an unbalanced element into life. When man began to think of himself as the center of the universe, he became like

God. But it was all a lie. Man is not the center of the universe, and he cannot be.

But as you trace the course of human history you can see that this is the seductive lie that the serpent has whispered into the ears of men ever since: "You are the center of life. This is your world, everything relates to you. What you like is right; what you don't like is wrong. What you want to do is right; don't let anyone make you do what you don't want to do. You are the center of things." You can find this idea throbbing and pulsating throughout the philosophies of men, that man stands at the center of things.

That is the curse that fell upon man when he ate of the fruit in the garden of Eden. In a psychedelic way his mind was twisted and he thought of himself as God, and related all things to himself. But when man does this he introduces an eccentric element into life, into creation. The problem with our unbalanced world today is that we have an earth filled with several billion eccentrics! That is why everything is always going off in wrong directions.

But the glory of the gospel is that when men are redeemed through faith in Jesus Christ they resume a balanced life, and everything relates once again to God. God now becomes the center of things. Though we may struggle to learn this, eventually all the thrust and purpose of the gospel are here, to put God back into the center of his world and relate everything in our life and in the lives of others to him and not to us. It does not make any difference how things affect us. The important thing is, what do they do to God? What is his relationship to these things?

Let me illustrate that with two stories I heard when I

was in Guatemala. Some friends and I were driving about Guatemala, visiting the old capital city, Antigua, with its lush tropical vegetation in its marvelous setting at the foot of three volcanoes. As we were going about the city my friends told me these two stories.

Several years ago, a mutual friend of ours had been killed in an automobile accident. Although my narrator had not been with him when he was killed, she came to the death scene and saw how the car was badly torn and mutilated in the accident. As the highway patrol examined the car they saw that the two men in the front seat, Dick and Victor, had not fastened their seatbelts. One of the investigators, an expert in this field, made the comment that if these men had fastened their seatbelts, Victor would have been killed instead of Dick.

My friend had occasion to tell Dick's widow of these circumstances, and her response was to cry out, "Why did this happen? Why was it Dick that was chosen, why did he have to die?" Then, as she watched the other man, Victor, in his ministry and saw how he was used and what a blessing he was to so many, even though she knew her husband was equally gifted, she faced this question and found that there was only one answer: God. It was God's choice, God's will. She said, "Who am I to tell him whom to choose? God has the right to make these decisions." Thus she related the most tragic event of her life to the central Being of history and found peace for a troubled heart.

The other story concerns Cameron Townsend, who founded Wycliffe Bible Translators many years ago in Guatemala. He came as a young man of twenty-one into the high mountains near Lake Atitlan and there began his translation work. From that simple beginning the worldwide ministry of Wycliffe Bible Translators has come. On the occasion of Wycliffe's fiftieth anniversary celebration in Guatemala, Cameron Townsend was there. He was highly honored by the government and people of Guatemala, and all of Central America. They had banquet after banquet in his name and he was given the highest honors which those countries were capable of bestowing. Everywhere he went he was feted and honored and his work exalted.

But my friend told me that, typically, Dr. Townsend turned every occasion into an opportunity to speak of the Lord Jesus Christ and of his work. Refusing the honor for himself, he related it to the One to whom it belonged. He put God into the center of things and maintained the balance of life.

This is what the Scripture means when it says that all of life must be built around the person of the Lord Jesus in order to make sense. There is coming a day when every knee shall bow, and every tongue confess that Jesus is Lord, to the glory of God the Father. Then the destruction, desolation, and heartache of the garden of Eden will be reversed, and men will once again acknowledge the centrality of God in life. Then the world will be filled with glory and righteousness from the river to the ends of the earth. Everything will be what God intended it to be.

But the glory of the gospel is that this can happen in human hearts right now. This is what the gospel message is all about. Have you ceased your rebellion against the will of God? Have you stopped trying to be a little god, trying to run things in your own home or office the way you want them to be? Have you crowned Jesus Christ Lord of his empire, where he belongs, and invited

him with gladness to sit upon the throne of your heart
and rule there? Have you stopped your grumbling and
complaining about all the things that come into your
life, that are his choice for you, and begun to rejoice as
the Scriptures exhort us, to "give thanks in all circumstances; for this is the will of God in Christ Jesus for
you"? (1 Thess. 5:18).

> *How we need this exhortation, our Father,*
> *to remind us of the one great theme of life:*
> *that life cannot, will not ever make sense, will*
> *not cease its endless friction, until it is related*
> *to the person of Jesus Christ our Lord. Grant*
> *that our hearts may each crown him anew*
> *Lord of Lords, King of Kings, and mean it—*
> *to live each day in that holy relationship. We*
> *ask in his name, Amen.*

3 / The Making of Woman

As a man who lives with a wife, four daughters, and a mother-in-law, I approach the subject of understanding women with considerable timidity. In our home I am even grateful for a *mail*box out front! But in considering this subject I do not turn to experience, but to the wonderfully helpful words of Scripture. In the latter part of Genesis, this theme is brought before us, the making of woman, and the role of woman in marriage—for when God made a woman, marriage was born.

In these latitudinarian days we read occasionally in the papers of the "marriage" of homosexuals. What a pathetically shabby imitation of what God intended marriage to be! Marriage involves a man and a woman, and this passage reveals to us three very helpful things relating to women and to marriage. In the first part we shall see the intent of God in making woman; then there follows a significant description of the process which he followed; and then the qualities of true marriage that result from the making of woman are outlined. Let us first turn to the intent of God:

Then the Lord God said, "It is not good that the man should be alone; I will make him

41

a helper fit for him." So out of the ground the Lord God formed every beast of the field and every bird of the air, and brought them to the man to see what he would call them; and whatever the man called every living creature, that was its name. The man gave names to all cattle, and to the birds of the air, and to every beast of the field; but for the man there was not found a helper fit for him (Gen. 2:18–20).

The first thing that is clear from this passage is that woman was made to be man's *companion*. "It is not good that the man should be alone." We know today that one of the most shattering emotions human beings experience is loneliness. When God pronounced a sentence of "not good" upon man's condition it was the interjection of the first negative element in the story of creation. Until then, everything had been pronounced good, and on the sixth day of creation God said that everything he had done was "very good." But now we read that it was not good for man to be alone, indicating that it never was God's intention for man to be alone, that from the very beginning he intended to make two sexes.

For a man or woman to exist in loneliness is always a devastating threat to the happiness and welfare of that individual. Loneliness is now reckoned to be the single greatest cause of suicide in this country, and it is undoubtedly the most widespread source of human misery in the world today. Yet it is a perfectly human experience. Each of us has felt at times the need for human companionship. There is nothing wrong with that; God made us that way. We need one another. We were not made to exist in loneliness.

I once heard John R. W. Stott of London, England, point out from the close of Paul's second letter to Timothy how lonely Paul was. Mr. Stott described the apostle as he sat in his tiny dungeon in Rome, with a circular opening in the ceiling above him as the only access, and how he informed Timothy that all had forsaken him and he begged the young man to come to him soon, before winter if possible, and to bring with him certain articles of clothing, books, and parchments, because he was cold in body, bored in mind, and lonely in spirit. Mr. Stott brought out what a perfectly human reaction this was. Despite the fact that the apostle could look beyond, that his departure was near at hand, and he was about to join the Lord in glory, and though he was thrilled with the possibilities that opened before him, yet this did not cancel out the human element of loneliness.

Now God knows that we need one another, and he provides others for us. It is clear from this passage that the chief, although not the sole answer, to the loneliness of man is the making of woman; man and woman together in marriage. One of the primary purposes of marriage is to provide companionship, a sharing of life together. I read recently that one of the famous actresses of the stage, the skilled and popular Gertrude Lawrence, once announced to her friends that she would like to get married. They said, "Why? You have everything that anyone could want. You have fame, close friends, abundant social life. What could marriage add to you?" She said, "It is because I want so desperately to have someone to nudge." She highlighted the need for companionship and the fact that this is an elementary hunger in human life.

Designed to Help

The second intent of God was that woman should be a *helper* to man, someone to share not only his life as a companion but his work and responsibilities as well. Man and woman are to work together in the building of a home and a life. It is interesting that this has been true from the very beginning of man's existence: men and women designed to work together. Perhaps there is nothing more destructive to marriage than the commonly held attitude that the man has his area of responsibility, his realm of life, such as his work, and the woman has hers—the home, the children—and there is little or no sharing together in these areas. It is always a destructive element in any home or marriage for either mate to hold out for a private realm to the exclusion of the other. The man has nothing much to say around the home; the woman has nothing to do with her husband's work. This is terribly wrong.

It is clear from this passage that God made woman to be a helper to man and to share with him a mutual concern and responsibility, though they may have different assignments according to the nature of their work. The nature of the work that supports a home and the level of living is to be primarily determined by the husband, but the decisions by which these are carried out and the labor involved is shared equally by the wife. This is made clear in this reference to woman as man's helper. But it is made even clearer by the remarkable verse that follows.

Here we have what logicians call a *non sequitur*, something that apparently has no relationship to what has gone before; it does not seem to follow. We have just read that God intends to make "*a helper fit for him*," which of course must be a woman, and then we read:

> So out of the ground the Lord God formed every beast of the field and every bird of the air, and brought them to the man to see what he would call them; and whatever the man called every living creature, that was its name (Gen. 2:19).

What has that to do with making a woman? How does that follow God's declaration of intent to make a helper for man? Obviously there must be a connection here. God set Adam to the task of studying the animals. He gave him a project to work out before he was ready for marriage. Doubtless it was in order to show him that his wife was to be quite different from the animals. Many men have not learned that yet, but it is clear that this was the intent of God in setting man out upon this search.

Now what did he learn as he examined the animals? Adam could not possibly have given names to the animals without knowing the character of each, because a name always reflects a characteristic. In the giving of a name to each of the animals Adam had to understand, whether by a revelation from God or by searching and examining on his own, something of the character of each animal. There are several things immediately evident that Adam learned in his study.

Pertaining to Animals

Perhaps first, he learned that woman was not to be a mere beast of burden as she has so often become in the history of the race since. There are societies where women are treated exactly like animals, where the price of a woman is approximately the price of a cow, and where women are sometimes traded for cows. But this is a violation of what Adam learned in the beginning, that woman is not like the animals. Adam did not find in the animals a helper fit for him. His wife, when she appeared, was quite different.

Therefore woman is not to be treated as a slave whose function begins and ends with household work. For a man to treat his wife as though she were only a servant or housekeeper, there only to keep everything in order, is devastating to her personality. Perhaps the most frequent cause of complaint from women in marriage is a variation on the theme: "He looks upon me just like another thing around the house. I'm like part of the furniture." This is terribly destructive to a woman's psychological make-up.

Second, Adam unquestionably learned in his search that woman is not to be merely a biological laboratory for the producing of children. Obviously it is women who bear children, but they are not to be like the animals who bear progeny as almost their sole reason for existence. Women are not to be like that. Sex has a much higher function in human life than the mere reproduction of children. One of the most destructive ideas that has been spread among mankind has been the teaching that the first and primary reason for marriage is the production of children. The Bible does not reflect that at all. There is in the Bible ample justification for birth control when circumstances warrant, and man has come to understand this under the terrible pressure of an exploding population that has made him face up squarely to the fact that woman was never intended to be merely a baby factory.

Third, Adam probably learned in his search that woman is not a "thing" outside himself. Women are not beasts of burden, they are not simply for producing children, and they are not something to be used at the whim of man and then disposed of. They are to be a helper fit for him, corresponding to him. Much of the current philosophy of life reflects the idea that women are nothing more than playthings for man—disposable women— you use them as you would use a Kleenex and then toss them away. But this passage directly contradicts that. Woman is to be a helper and a companion, fit for man, corresponding exactly and continuously to his needs, constantly able to adjust to the changes that come in to his life.

Let us move on to consider briefly the process which God followed in making woman:

> So the Lord God caused a deep sleep to fall upon the man, and while he slept took one of his ribs and closed up its place with flesh; and the rib which the Lord God had taken from the man he made into a woman and brought her to the man (Gen. 2:21,22).

This most interesting account has been derided and laughed at as being literally impossible, yet those who deride it forget that they are reckoning with an almighty God. A scientist told me once that it is quite possible for any cell of the body potentially to reproduce, not only itself, but the member of which it is a part, and even ultimately the whole body. I have not looked into that further but if that is the case then there is certainly no problem involved in God actually taking a rib and using it to make a woman. It is absurd to argue as some do that this could not have happened because men have the same number of ribs as women do today. After all, if you cut off your finger it does not mean that your children will be born minus a finger.

But there are two things about this that are very significant. First, there is the revelation that man was caused to fall into a deep sleep and woman was made during this period of unconsciousness. These things are reported to us not only because they actually happened but because they also are suggestive of certain continuing relationships that obtain. This period of unconsciousness strongly suggests what modern psychology also confirms, that the relationships of marriage, the ties between a man and his wife, are far deeper than mere surface affection. They are a part, not only of the conscious life of man, but of the unconscious, the subconscious.

This explains what any marriage counselor soon recognizes: why it is that men and women are so puzzled by one another's reactions at times. They know that they themselves are often upset or angry or hurt at something the other one has done, but they can't put their finger on the reason. It is, of course, because the other person has violated a basic drive which God himself has built into the feminine or masculine nature and which is rooted in the basic nature of each individual. Though we cannot put our finger on what is bothering us, we know there is something wrong. This is why Peter in his first letter exhorts the man to dwell with his wife "according to knowledge" (1 Pet. 3:7, KJV). The responsibility of the man in marriage is to understand what the Scriptures teach about women, and to help his wife to understand herself as well as to understand him. She will have a much easier task understanding him than she does herself.

Close to the Heart

The second revelation here is that woman was made from a rib. Sceptics laugh at this, but God knew what he was doing. It is most significant that a rib was chosen from which to make woman. The rib emphasizes the essentially emotional nature of women. Ribs are the bones nearest the heart, and are thus closely linked with the heart. Throughout Scripture it is always the heart which is pictured as the center of emotional life.

This emotional character of woman is confirmed by modern psychology. Tears, fears, and cheers come more easily to women than they do to men. In this, woman is designed to complete man, to be a helper fit for him. It is this very emotional nature which adds color and warmth to life. How drab life would be without it.

The second significant aspect of the rib is that it emphasizes the protective instinct in women. It is the rib which protects the vital organs of the chest and notably the heart. In fact, the Hebrew word for "helper" is the word *azar*, which means "to surround." Just as the rib cage surrounds the heart and protects it, so there is in woman an instinctive reaction of protectiveness. Anyone who has tried to come between a man and his wife, or to abuse a man to his wife, knows what I mean. C. S. Lewis has pointed this out in asking the question, "If your dog has bitten a neighbor's child, would you rather face the mother or the father to discuss the issue?"

So the process of God in making woman reveals that she is to be a companion and a helper, by utilizing to the full her inherent emotional and protective instincts. Now we come to the qualities of marriage that result from the union of man and woman:

> Then the man said, "This at last is bone of my bones and flesh of my flesh; she shall be called Woman, because she was taken out of Man." Therefore a man leaves his father and his mother and cleaves to his wife, and they become one flesh. And the man and his wife were both naked, and were not ashamed (Gen. 2: 23–25).

This is a very remarkable passage because it encompasses in brief all the great concepts of marriage that run throughout the rest of the Bible. They are all condensed and encapsulated in these few verses. When God had finished making woman and Adam had slept off the deep unconsciousness into which he had fallen, God brought the woman to Adam. What a scene that must have been! Here is the first of a long, long series of boy meets girl stories. Out of the highly condensed account of this encounter there emerge four factors essential to true marriage.

One Flesh

The first and most fundamental of all is that marriage is to involve a complete identity of the partners; two are to be one. Adam's first reaction when he saw his wife was, "This at last is bone of my bones and flesh of my flesh," that is, she is one being with me. This is strengthened in the latter part of verse twenty-four where it adds, "and they become one flesh." It is not without reason that this has become part of the marriage service, this recognition of unity. As someone has well said, the one word above all that makes marriage successful is "ours." Things belong to "us." "Bone of my bones and flesh of my flesh." Thus, as the New Testament so wisely points out, the man who hurts his wife is hurting himself. He may not feel it directly, but down the line the result of it will show in his life, because she is really, genuinely, and factually sharing one life with him. They become one flesh. This is not poetry; it is reality.

Two people become one when they are married, and as their life goes on together, there is a blending of psyches, a merging of lives, and the creating of a single history. It is for this reason that divorce is such a terrible thing, especially after years of marriage. It is the severing of a person. It is butchery, the dividing up of a single life, much as you would take an axe and split a body in two. No wonder it is so terribly painful—much more deeply felt than those who experience it understand at the time.

The second thing that is brought out here is the biblical principle of headship, which is developed at much greater length in the New Testament. "She shall be called woman, because she was taken out of man." Paul enlarges on this in his letter to the Corinthians, to point out that man was not made for woman but woman was made for man (1 Cor. 11:9). It is the man who is ultimately responsible before God for the nature and character of the home. It is the man who must exercise leadership in determining the direction in which the home should go, and must therefore answer for that leadership, or its lack, before God. The woman's responsibility is to acknowledge this leadership.

One of the most serious threats to marriage and one of the primary causes of divorce in our day, is the fact that men are abdicating the role of leadership in the home, leaving it up to the wife to raise the children. They are refusing to be fathers to their children and husbands to their wives, wanting rather to be sons to another mother and to have their own needs ministered to.

The third factor indicated here which characterizes true marriage is permanence. "Therefore a man leaves his father and his mother and cleaves to his wife." This is a strong word. In the Hebrew text it is the word, *dabag*, which means "to adhere firmly, as if with glue," to be lovingly devoted to a wife. In the days of Henry Ford and the Model T, someone asked him to what formula he attributed his successful marriage. He said, "The same formula as the making of a successful car: stick to one model." That is exactly what is said in this passage. A husband is to cleave to his wife. He forsakes all others and adheres to her. Whatever she may be like, he is to hold to her. He is to stay with her, and she with him, because marriage is a permanent bond.

Nothing to Hide

Finally, the fourth factor is set forth in this verse: "And the man and his wife were both naked, and were not ashamed." This speaks clearly of openness between a man and wife—literally, nothing to hide. They have no secrets, nothing that they do not share with each other. It is the failure to achieve this kind of openness that lies behind so much breakdown in marriage, the utter lack of communication, where two sit and look at one another and say nothing. They may talk about merely surface trivialities, but there is no discussion of their problems or what they are thinking on various issues. This is often why they are so judgmental with one another, each one trying to get the other to agree and not being willing to allow differences of viewpoint to exist.

But openness does not mean agreeing or feeling the same. It means a readiness to share with one another, completely, without insisting that the other reflect the same attitude. There is room here for ultimate decisions and the submitting of a wife to the leadership of the husband. Openness does not cancel that out. But there is to be a complete freedom of communication, one with the other. Marriages shrivel, wither, and die when this is not true.

What is the result of all this? In Eden these four principles were at work. Adam and Eve were united as one. There was the recognition of the principle of headship. Adam had the right to make ultimate decisions in all matters. They intended to be together permanently and Adam was responsible for this. There was an openness between them so that they hid nothing from one another. What was the result? The text says, "they were not ashamed." Well if they were not ashamed, what were they? What is the opposite of being ashamed? It is to be relaxed. We would use the term, well-adjusted. They felt at ease with each other. There was no strain in their marriage. They were fully at ease with one another. Is that not what we strive for in marriage? These are the principles that produce it.

There is God's design for marriage. As we hold it

before us we can see by contrast the reasons why so many marriages are failing. What we need desperately is to return to this biblical pattern, for here are revealed the secrets of happy married life.

As always, Father, we feel the searching quality of your word as it seeks us out and exposes to us the weakness of our lives and the wrongness of our attitudes. But it sets before us also, so beautifully, the great possibilities of our lives, the potential that awaits us when we are willing to submit ourselves to the wisdom that is reflected in your word. Grant to us now submissive hearts and restored confidence in one another. Make our homes happy ones, where children are delighted to stay home and share times of fellowship with their father and mother, where friends look forward to coming, where peace, harmony, and joy prevail, and grace is manifest in every day's activities. We ask it in Jesus' name, Amen.

4 / The Enticement of Evil

It is with a heightened sense of anticipation that we come to chapter three of Genesis. In many ways this is the most important piece of information ever conveyed to man. Here is the ultimate explanation for the tensions and conflicts that are constantly flaring up around the world. Here we have the answer to the eternal "why" that arises in our hearts in times of tragedy or sorrow. Here is the explanation for over a hundred centuries of human heartache, misery, torture, blood, sweat, and tears. Here is the reason for the powerful fascination that drugs hold for young people today; the passion for power; the lure of wealth; and the enticements of forbidden sex, to young and old alike. Here is the only reasonable answer for the existence of all these things in the world today.

If you remove this chapter from the Bible, the rest of it is absolutely incredible. Ignore the teaching of this chapter in history and the story of humanity becomes impossible either to understand or to explain. The most striking thing about Genesis three is that you and I find ourselves here. You can't read through this story without feeling that you have lived it yourself, because you have.

The temptation and the fall are reproduced in our lives many times a day. We have all heard the voice of the Tempter. We have all felt the drawing of sin. We know the pangs of guilt that follow.

This is why many call this story a myth. In the sense that it is timeless truth, perhaps that word has certain rationality. But there are other implications of the term myth which make it unsuitable to apply to this account. It is timeless in the sense that this is always happening to mankind, but it is timeless only because it is also fact. It actually did occur. It happens continually because it did happen once to our original parents and thus, we, their children, cannot escape repeating it. In that sense there is no chapter in the Bible that is more up-to-date and more pertinent to our own situation than this one.

The Shining One

Let us look at the Tempter himself and the first point of the strategy that he employs. The Tempter is introduced in the first sentence of verse one:

> Now the serpent was more subtle than any other wild creature that the Lord God had made (Gen. 3:1).

I am very sorry that this word in the Hebrew was ever translated "serpent," because it has given rise to a very false idea about this story—that there was in the garden of Eden a talking snake. I have no doubt in my mind that if God chose to make a snake talk, he could. I accept fully the other account in the Bible of a talking animal, when God opened the mouth of Balaam's ass and spoke to the prophet through the donkey. I have no problem with this. Even man can teach animals to talk and surely God can do so.

But the interesting thing is that this account does not really say that there was a snake in the garden of Eden. The Hebrew word here is *Nachash* which means literally "to shine," or in the noun form here, a "shining one." If you read it that way, an entirely different being emerges:

> Now the shining one was more subtle than any other wild creature that the Lord God had made.

Thus, the first description that we have of the Tempter is that he appeared to Eve as a shining one. Undoubtedly, snakes were created to represent this being who appeared in the garden as the shining one, as other kinds of animals represent certain characteristics of people. For instance, in the rest of Scripture we can see that wolves were deliberately designed by God to represent and symbolize rapacious human beings, vicious people. Sheep, I believe, were designed deliberately by God to represent believers. If you ever get to feeling proud of yourself, go study some sheep for awhile. (I come from Monta-a-a-a-na and feel somewhat of an expert in this area.) And it is clear from the Scriptures that pigs were designed by God to symbolize unbelievers, unregenerate people.

It is no wonder then that snakes have become an almost universal symbol of Satan. But here it was not a snake that appeared but a shining one, of whom snakes have become symbols. You will recall that Paul in his second letter to the Corinthians speaks of Satan as "an angel of light" (2 Cor. 11:14). So it was the *Nachash* that appeared, the shining one. He is also called in the Book of Revelation that "old serpent," the original serpent, the Devil. There is thus no question about the identity of the one who suddenly appears here.

It is the Devil in his character as an angel of light, a shining being, all glorious to behold, who now confronts the woman in the garden of Eden. He is the being whom Jesus Christ called "the ruler of this world." He is the one whom Paul refers to as "the god of this age," the malevolent being who is behind the philosophy of men, who dominates the thinking of the world, who has the ear of humanity and whispers into it a lie, an outrageous but very attractive lie, that makes men drool with desire. This is the one of whom Martin Luther properly said, "On earth is not his equal." No man is able to outwit the Devil. He has defeated the greatest saints of God at times throughout all of history, except for the son of God himself.

We are also told here that he was "more subtle than any other wild creature" (literally, *living* creature). The word *subtle* means crafty or cunning. His craftiness is evident right from the beginning in that he sought out the woman. It was a desire to play on her emotional nature that led the Devil to seek out the woman and to begin his temptation with her. He comes, as he always does, in disguise. He never appears with horns, hooves, and a tail, announcing that he is Satan. If he came that way, everyone would reject him. No one wants to be evil, in that open, defiant sense. But the Devil is disguised, appearing to be not bad but good, a shining being of wholesome character and benevolent purpose.

The Devil Is Limited

Let us move on to consider the strategy which the Tempter employs. It is exactly the strategy he uses on us—not that we shall see visions of shining beings, but the personality he exemplifies, the character in which he appears, is the same now as then. Scripture makes clear that the Devil can also appear as a roaring lion, he can strike in tragedy, in sickness, in physical evil, as he did to Job or to the Apostle Paul with his thorn in the flesh which Paul called the messenger of Satan. Or, as a lion, he can strike fear into our hearts. But his most effective strategy is to appear as something or someone who appeals to us as an angel of light; as such, his strategy is always the same.

This is actually encouraging. If you learn how to recognize the strategy of the Devil, you will find that he invariably employs the same tactics. In a sense, the Devil is very limited. He doesn't vary his tactics widely. Sometimes we feel we will never learn how to anticipate the Devil. But we can learn. The Apostle Paul said that he was not ignorant of the Devil's devices. If we learn how he works, we can easily detect him in our lives.

As a matter of fact, the Apostle James has described this strategy very plainly in one or two verses:

> Each person is tempted when he is lured
> and enticed by his own desire. Then desire
> when it has conceived gives birth to sin; and
> sin when it is full-grown brings forth death
> (Jas. 1:14,15).

There is the strategy of the Devil. It is his strategy here in the garden of Eden and it is his strategy in your life and mine. The only difference between us and Eve in the garden is that for her the Tempter stood outside. She was innocent and he stood outside attempting to reach into her mind and thoughts. Since the fall, the Tempter is within us and has access to us so that we are never out of reach of temptation. We are always exposed. We can go a thousand miles away but we will never be able to avoid temptation. We carry a tempter within us wherever we go.

Yet he always approaches us in the same three stages and those steps are outlined clearly in this passage from James. His first tactic is to arouse desire. James says that every man "is tempted when he is lured and enticed by his own desire." The first step the Devil takes with us is always to arouse desire to do wrong, to create a hunger, a lure or enticement toward evil. The second is to permit intent to form and an act to occur. As James describes it, "desire when it has conceived gives birth to sin."

Notice that the symbol he employs is that of conception and birth. There is a gestation period in temptation, for once desire is aroused there occurs a process which sooner or later issues in sin, an act that is wrong. The third stage is that the Devil immediately acts upon the opportunity afforded by the evil act to move in and to produce results which Scripture describes as "death." "Sin when it is full-grown brings forth death."

This is the Devil's ultimate aim. Jesus said that Satan was a murderer from the beginning. He delights in mangling, smashing, twisting, destroying, blighting, and blasting. We can see his activity present everywhere; it is going on around us, in our own lives, and in the lives of others. These are "the works of the Devil," says the

Scripture. He brings them about by the process we see in this story.

For the moment, we will consider only the first stage of this process. Let us watch now how the Tempter cunningly moves to arouse desire within Eve's heart.

> He said to the woman, "Did God say, 'You shall not eat of any tree of the garden'?" And the woman said to the serpent, "We may eat of the fruit of the trees of the garden; but God said, 'You shall not eat of the fruit of the tree which is in the midst of the garden, neither shall you touch it, lest you die.'" But the serpent said to the woman, "You will not die. For God knows that when you eat of it your eyes will be opened, and you will be like God, knowing good and evil" (Gen. 3:1–5).

His first task is to make the woman want to sin. That is not very difficult with us. We respond quite readily to these desires, these urges within us to do wrong. But it was quite a different story with Eve. Remember, at this time she was innocent, she trusted and loved God. She felt no wrong desire springing up from within her, such as we must wrestle with. The Tempter had to awaken a wrong desire in her heart. His opportunity was provided by the gift of free will which God has given to man. This helps to explain the question that many ask: "How is it that the Devil was allowed access to the garden of Eden in the first place? Why does the Tempter appear in this story? How did he get into the garden?"

The only possible answer of course is that God allowed him to come in. He was permitted to come. He

came with the full knowledge and consent of God because it was necessary that man be tempted. He must be
able to respond *voluntarily* to God. The greatest gift
God has given to us is the ability to make moral choices;
we have the right to be wrong if we insist. God himself
does not violate this. He does not coerce us. He does not
force us to be right. We have the right to reject his love,
and the right to turn off his grace, refuse his mercy, and
go our own stubborn way. God allows that to be. It is
the greatest dignity given to man.

Many people struggle with this. They say, "Why
doesn't God make us behave?" Well, if he did, he would
have taken away this great dignity. These same people
are the ones who say, "Well, I don't want anyone telling
me what to do. I want to make up my own mind." But
you can't have it both ways. Because God is a God of
love—and love never coerces, never forces someone to
love in return—it is absolutely essential that man be
given the chance to choose whether he wants to continue to love God or to go another direction. So the
Tempter comes into the garden and because of the gift
of free will he is given the opportunity to tempt the
woman. Free will is that which makes us men, but it is
also what makes us temptable. Even the Lord Jesus
faced this same relationship. He was given the gift of
free choice, too, and therefore he was exposed to the
power of Satan.

Seed of Doubt

Now notice that in trying to arouse desire in this
woman the Tempter follows a threefold plan. This
again is very instructive to us, because it is the same way
in which he will move with us. His first step was to im-

plant distrust in her heart, a distrust of God's love. He raised the question, "Did God say you shall not eat of any tree of the garden?" He means by this obviously, "Could God have said a thing like that, really? How well do you know him? Do you think that a God who loves you would ask you not to eat of a tree of the garden?"

With that question he plants a seed of doubt in the woman's heart. He is seeking to alter the image of God in her thinking. He is saying in effect, "Either you misunderstood him and he didn't really say that, or if he did say it, he obviously is not quite the kind of a God that you have imagined him to be." With this single question he casts a small cloud over Eve's trust in God, and the response of love in her heart. Could God really have said a thing like that?

Have you ever heard this question? Can a God who loves you forbid anything to you? Is it really love if he forbids something? The question hangs over the whole human race and has done so ever since this first occasion in the garden.

You will notice that the woman's answer is perfectly forthright, without guile. She says immediately,

> "We may eat of the fruit of the trees of the garden; but God said, 'You shall not eat of the fruit of the tree which is in the midst of the garden, neither shall you touch it, lest you die.'"

There are some who have attempted to accuse the woman of adding to God's statement when she says, "Neither shall you touch it," because that was not part of the prohibition given in verse seventeen of chapter two. I do not think we need to view it that way. No doubt the woman is giving a fuller account of what God had said. Very likely he did say, "You shall not touch it." God is thereby saying, "Look, this tree is harmful and therefore don't get near it. Don't expose yourself to its temptation."

Most impressively in the Lord's Prayer we are taught to pray, "Lead us not into temptation." Notice the prayer does not say, "Lead me out of temptation once I have gotten into it." No, by the time we have gotten into it, we are already half lost. When we feel the raging of desire within us, it is a late hour to start praying. The Lord teaches us to pray beforehand, "Lead me not even into the realm of temptation. Don't let me come to the place where I shall feel this tremendous arousing and awakening of desire within."

Point of Limitation

Notice that temptation always comes to us at this point of limitation. God said to the man and the woman, "Here is an area in which I must limit you. There is only this one place. The whole world is yours, the whole planet. You may eat of any fruit, any tree, anywhere, except for this one tree." Haven't you discovered that God is forever saying this to us also, in one way or another? In this sense, the tree of good and evil is still right in the midst of the garden of our lives. Wherever we may turn we are confronted by the fact that we are limited in some way. The testing of our humanity is whether we are willing to accept and abide by the limitations God puts upon us.

As a child, are you willing to accept the authority of your parents in the home? As a student, are you willing to accept the fact that you are not a mature person yet that you can't make the rules of life, for you are still learning them?

As a married woman, are you willing to accept the authority of a husband in your life? Are you willing to recognize that God has made a distinction between the sexes and that the man is given a role of leadership that the woman does not have? That is the testing place in your life. As a man, are you willing to accept the fact that you are a man and not God? That there are things you cannot know and mysteries which you can't yet explore?

You are not an infinite being; you are a finite creature. You don't know everything. You must sit at the feet of God and listen to his voice and learn from him. You are not equipped with all that it takes to explore life adequately. You are a man. Are you willing to accept that limitation? Throughout the whole history of our race the violation of this limitation has brought sorrow, heartache, and misery.

Now see how the Tempter moves in quickly. He now dares to deny openly the results that God has stated will occur. "You will not die," he says. He openly substitutes a lie for the truth, but he does it in the realm of the future where you can't check the results. Notice his cleverness here as he says, "It is not going to happen as God says. Don't take God so seriously. Surely these issues are not that important. If God is a God of love, then this can't be a life or death matter. After all, don't make a federal case out of this! It is really rather trivial."

Do you see how this is repeated in life today? It is so easy to say, "These things are simple matters which have to deal only with secondary issues of life. This is not what the Bible says it is—a life or death matter—at least you can't take it that way if you believe in a God who loves you." So the Devil cleverly uses the great truths about the being and character of God to plant a doubt in this woman's heart, and to support it with an outright lie, declaring that what God had predicted would not happen.

Then notice the third step. Quickly he moves in to support his lie with a distorted truth. If we look closely at the many cults of our day, we can see that every false faith is made up of a certain amount of truth—ten percent error and ninety percent truth, mixed together. But ultimately it is the ten percent of error that leads men astray. This is exactly the Devil's tactic here. He said to Eve,

> God knows that when you eat of it your
> eyes will be opened, and you will be like God,
> knowing good and evil.

Now that was perfectly true. Look at verse seven of this same chapter. "Then the eyes of both were opened." And look also at verse twenty-two, "Then the Lord God said, 'Behold, the man has become like one of us, knowing good and evil.'"

This is exactly what the Devil said would happen. But with this difference. Their eyes *were* opened and they *did* become able to know good and evil as God knows it but they learned to relate everything to themselves. They used, as the measurement of good and evil, their own feelings. That is the way God does. But what the Devil didn't tell them was that this would be the most disastrous thing that could happen to them. They thought that the Devil meant something expansive, something glorious. But when their eyes were opened it was shameful, sordid, and sad. "Oh," you say, "how diabolically clever." Exactly! That is the way the Devil always works. Eyes are opened but not to what is expected.

But now the Devil is through with the woman. He has succeeded in arousing desire, and that is all he wants. The other two stages will almost certainly follow, and they do for Eve is now deceived. All the Devil wishes to do is to leave Eve standing before the fruit, hanging there in all its luscious fascination, tantalizing her, offering her an experience she never dreamed would be possible. He has planted the seed he wants in her heart. He has caused her to slightly distrust God's love, to believe a lie, and to expect an unwarranted result. That is all he needs to do. Now she stands aroused and deceived, in the presence of the fruit, and the Devil can safely leave her, even though she has not yet sinned. He is fully certain that the desired results will follow.

"Well," you say, "what went wrong here? How could she have avoided this? Where was the battle lost?" As you look through the account you can see that the battle was lost right after the first sentence, when he raised the question, "Did God say . . . ?" From the moment she mentally accepted the idea that God was not fully to be trusted, she was whipped, beaten, and lost. Immediately after that the Devil becomes bold and comes right out in the open to lie to her blatantly. And she believes him from then on.

Have you experienced this kind of thing? This is the process the Tempter uses when he tries to get you to have an affair with another man's wife or another woman's husband. This is the process he follows when he wants to get you involved in a shady business deal, or to cheat in an examination, or simply to tell a lie in your relationships with others.

God's Way—Satan's Way

The interesting thing about this is that there was nothing wrong in arousing desire in this woman's heart, because God does that too. God is at work also to arouse our desires, to make us want to do his will, to stimulate us and activate us, to move us out. The difference lies in the way he does it. If we don't get anything else out of this story we will have learned a tremendous lesson if we can differentiate between the ways God and the Devil arouse desire in the heart of man.

How does God do it? First, he demonstrates his love to us. That is always God's first approach. He comes and touches us somehow, blesses us, pours out upon us his sunshine and his rain, all the blessings of our lives. He comes in Christ and moves in among us and lives with us, blessing us. He gives himself.

Second, he declares a promised result. He gives his word to us. He declares what will happen. He opens to us a new vista of what life can be like. Third, he offers us his presence to bring about the fulfillment of that promise. Jesus said, "Come unto me," and "If any one hears my voice and opens the door, I will come in to him" (Rev. 3:20). God offers to enter life personally and to be with us. This leads on to fulfillment, to blessing, to joy, and oneness.

Do you see the contrast between the way God works and the way the Devil works? The Devil first implants a distrust of God's love; the Lord *demonstrates* his love. God *declares* a promise to us; the Devil declares a countering lie. God strengthens his promise by offering himself, the truth itself, to us. The Devil distorts that truth and makes it look like something else, makes it vague and undefined. That is the way you can tell the difference.

Are you being tempted to do wrong, take a course that is wrong, make a decision that will lead to death or disaster down the line? How do you know whether it is from God or Satan? It all looks so good, doesn't it? Well, ask yourself these questions. Do I feel cheated, deprived, or limited right now? Do I feel as though God is somehow holding out on me, that I am not being given all that I ought to have, that my rights are being violated, that I am being cheated of something life should give me? Well, then you are listening to the voice of the Tempter. That is his first approach. "Did God say this? Would a God who loves you say a thing like that? Would he hold out on you? Would he postpone the blessing he wants you to have?"

Then ask yourself if what you want contradicts the truth that God has revealed. Can you find in the Scriptures that what you are after, what you are seeking, is wrong, yet all the world is telling you that it is right and that it will bring you blessing? Does the Word of God stand in opposition to what you are after? Then you are listening again to the Tempter's voice, for he lies, outrightly, blatantly. He says the results will be different from what the revealed word says.

Finally ask yourself if the promised result is rather vague and uncertain. Is it just a general promise of blessing or happiness; or is it specific—clearly and precisely defined? If it is unspecific, you are listening again to the voice of the Tempter. This is why the Scripture comes back again and again to this simple theme:

> Trust in the Lord with all your heart, and do
> not rely on your own insight (Prov. 3:5).

You are but men, only human. You don't know all there is to know about life. You can't know. There isn't anyone who knows. You desperately need the revelation of truth which can come from God alone. No one else can supply it. No other book will give you the answers. There is no other place where you can find out what life is all about except in the Word of God. Therefore, "Trust in the Lord with all your heart, and do not rely on your own insight. In all your ways acknowledge him, and he will make straight your paths" (Prov. 3:5,6).

> How long it has taken us, Father, to learn
> the truths that are declared to us in this pas-
> sage. How ignorant we have been. What
> dupes, what stupid victims we have been of
> the Devil's lies, so many times in our lives.
> How foolish we have been to distrust your
> love, to believe that you who love us could tell
> us a lie. Father, open our eyes; help us to see
> that the only place of fulfillment, the only
> place of happiness, the only place of joy, is in
> a heart that trusts and completely rests with
> quiet acceptance upon your love and grace. In
> Jesus' name, Amen.

5 / The Heart of Temptation

We have watched Eve in the garden of Eden being assaulted in mind and will by the Tempter. As a shining one he appeared to her and sought to arouse a desire in her for the forbidden fruit. The basic nature of temptation, then, is always a pressure upon us to exceed the limitations which God has placed upon us. God has established these limitations for us, not out of cruelty or unkindness, but out of love and grace. They are necessary to our humanity. But the character of temptation is to make use of this limitation, to make us restive and discontented so that we will be drawn out beyond the limits.

With Eve, the Tempter actually accomplished this by first creating a sense of unfairness in her. This is most revealing in the light of the situation we find so widespread today when many are seething in a ferment of discontent and restlessness, suffering (often justifiably) from a sense of being treated unfairly, but allowing that resentment to take control of the thought and mind. The Tempter has created a sense of unfairness, Eve's mind was prepared to receive the lie that God is not trustworthy and does not really love. The third step

71

was to present to her an incomplete and misleading statement of truth; to twist it, distort it slightly. Thus her desire was aroused for the forbidden fruit.

Now stage two occurs. In many ways this is the most important of all. Before this stage was reached it would have been quite possible for Eve to resist the temptation that had been aroused within her, but after this point it becomes more difficult; in fact, practically impossible. This stage is given to us in one verse:

> So when the woman saw that the tree was good for food, and that it was a delight to the eyes, and that the tree was desired to make one wise, she took of its fruit and ate; and she also gave some to her husband, and he ate (Gen. 3:6).

Up to this point the Tempter has worked upon Eve's feelings and aroused a strong desire within her for the forbidden thing. But now the mind must come into action. It is the function of the mind to pass upon the logic of the situation.

Our mental faculties are a tremendous gift from God. Basically they are the ability to reflect on circumstances and facts, and relate our attitude or activity to these. There is a logicality that must prevail. The question of the mind is always: Is the action about to be taken, or the attitude about to be formed, a rational one? Is it consistent with the facts?

Rationality demands that the whole man become involved, that one acts as a total being. Irrationality, or insanity, is the action of a person based on only part of his being—only his emotions, or even the direct activity of the will, apart from the exercise of mind or emotions.

But rationality insists that the total man be involved, so the mind must come into play.

The Deadly Power

At this point, therefore, the mind of Eve is engaged. But a terrible thing has already happened to her. She does not realize it, but it is evident from this account that the arousing of her emotion, the strong desire to have this fruit which hangs there in all its tantalizing mystery, has already prepared her will to act. Even before her mind comes into play she wants the fruit and has secretly determined to have it.

Thus, when her mind comes into action it can no longer do so rationally. It cannot consider the facts as they are, but must act on the facts as they appear to her. Since it can no longer act rationally it must rationalize. That is the deadly power of the mind in man. It has an amazing ability to rationalize, to twist the facts so that they accord with desire, to satisfy the urge that is springing up within by justifying it, even though doing so must slightly distort the facts of the situation.

Notice the process here. The first thing is that Eve looked at the fruit and said to herself, "It is good for food. It is something that will help me; it is physically profitable. Never mind the long-range effects—I'm not interested in that—it will satisfy a present and immediate need, and what can be wrong with that?"

Second, she saw that it was "a delight to the eyes," which means it was pleasurable, it satisfied the aesthetic sense. This element is always present in temptation. Each of us is well aware, because we are all experts in this, that sin is always fun—for awhile! It has an element of pleasure about it and there is no use trying to pretend otherwise. It is the pleasure of sin which makes it so enticing and alluring to us. The desire to have that pleasure, at whatever cost, is really the essential element of temptation.

It feels good to indulge myself. I love the feeling of splurging, of doing something that gives me pleasure. It feels great. That is why I do it, even though my mind may be telling me that it will be ultimately harmful. It feels good to act on pride. It satisfies me in some way. It feels good to lose my temper. Have you ever had the perverse delight of telling somebody off? Oh, how good that feels—for awhile! It feels good even though you do not do it to someone's face but go out in the woods to do it. Even that relieves the pain for a bit. It feels good to hurt my wife when she has done something that displeases me.

There is pleasure in sin, wherein lies the deceitfulness of sin. As Eve saw the fruit she said, "It is good for food, and it is a delight to the eyes. It is beautiful to look at."

Finally, she saw that it was "to be desired to make one wise." Thus, again, in the Book of James, we have a reference to the wisdom that is in view here. Desired to make one wise? Yes, says James, but there are two kinds of wisdom. There is the wisdom that is from above, from God; and there is a wisdom which is from below, which, he says, is "earthly, unspiritual, devilish" (Jas. 3:15). Paul wrote to the Corinthians that "the wisdom of the world is folly with God" (1 Cor. 3:19). But it appears to us to be alluring and satisfying.

John, in his first letter, says that there is a threefold appeal in the things the world values, which corresponds to the appeal of the fruit to Eve's physical, sensual, and ego-satisfying desires. He wrote:

> For all that is in the world, the *lust of the flesh* and the *lust of the eyes* and the *pride of life*, is not of the Father but is of the world (1 John 2: 16).

The tree was "good for food." That is John's "lust of the flesh." Then it was "a delight to the eyes." There is "the lust of the eyes." Finally, it was "desired to make one wise." And that is John's "pride of life." So much of the philosophy of the world is based upon this "pride of life." We must discover ways of building ourselves up, enhancing self, taking special courses by which we can develop the powers of our personality, or going to school to develop charm or poise. All of this is ministering to the pride of life, the satisfying of the ego—but is the snare of the Devil.

The Divine Order

Eve did not realize that her mind had played a trick upon her. It had taken the apparent facts which the enemy had set before her and had justified them, so that they looked reasonable, rational. The thing to do then, of course, was to give in. After all, anything that is good for food, pleasurable to the senses, and satisfying to the ego must be all right. But this is nothing less than a prostitution of the mind! It is reversing God's order.

In man as God made him, the order is to be, first, an appeal to the mind, then the stirring of the emotions based upon the facts presented to the mind; and then the two working together, the mind and emotions, to move the will. This is why, throughout the Scriptures, the appeal of the gospel, the good news from God, is addressed first to the mind.

The first appeal of the gospel is never to the emotions —it is always to the mind, to the understanding. It is a presentation of certain historic facts which have significance, and the significance of those facts is what constitutes the good news. Paul says, "I preached to you the gospel . . . that Christ died for our sins" (1 Cor. 15: 1,3). *He died,* (the fact); *for our sins,* (that is the significance of it); and *he rose again,* to be a living Lord imparting himself to us.

This is what constitutes the good news, that Christ died to solve the problem of our rebelliousness and our estrangement from God, and he rose again, to minister to us constantly of his life, of his grace, and of his strength. Upon these facts we can then make a decision. These facts move us and stir us—they ought to, they are designed to. But there must constantly come first the appeal to the mind. That is why any evangelism which does not begin with teaching is a false evangelism. Any evangelism which moves directly to an appeal to the will to act, or to the emotions to feel, is distorted and results in abortion instead of birth.

Now this technique of reversal prevails throughout the world. This is the technique of Madison Avenue and the advertising business. Thumb through a magazine and notice that all the advertisements are designed to arouse desire first. There sits a beautifully designed and painted sports car, displayed in living color. You cannot look at these beautiful advertisements without beginning to drool a bit. There is a color TV set, the color so real it is unbelievable. Then you look at your drab, black-and-white set in the corner, and you think "How can I put up with a thing like that any longer?" All showrooms and windows of stores are designed to short-circuit the mind and appeal first to the will through the emotions.

This is the technique of politicians and propagandists of every school. They too seek to arouse an emotional reaction first. They cleverly and carefully think through what will appeal to the emotions first and they start on that note. Someone wishes to move students, so he begins talking about war, the draft, or the curriculum. When the emotions are properly stirred, they present their plea for action, whatever the cause may be.

There are certain emotionally-charged words that immediately arouse blacks: civil rights, black power, and so on. To white middle classes, the propagandists talk about property values, free enterprise, and the "American way of life." By this sloganeering they attempt to arouse emotions first, with the realization that when the mind comes into play (as it will), it will not think rationally but will rationalize; it will take facts and distort them to justify the desire that has been aroused.

This explains why the propaganda to convince people of the hazard of cigarette smoking has been relatively ineffective. Cigarette smoking is not based upon rational observation. If it were, no one would smoke. Who wants lung cancer? But the only way by which the effects of cigarette advertising can be counteracted is by fighting fire with fire—by arousing emotions in the opposite direction. To that end, there has been a proliferation of articles on the terrible effects of throat and lung cancer.

All this is with the hope that the emotion of fear will turn people from the dangers of cigarette smoking. But why do people smoke? Why do boys begin to smoke? I remember my own boyhood and my attempts at smoking. Why? Because I thought that in some way it made me a man. In my desire to be a grown-up individual, it ministered to my sense of pride.

Now it would be entirely wrong to get the idea from this account that everything that is pleasurable is wrong, and everything that is right is boring, dull, and flat. That, of course, is what the enemy would like to have us believe about God; anything God wants for us is very dull, uninteresting, and lackluster, and the only exciting things are the things that are wrong.

For after all, it is God who designed our emotions. He made us to have feelings, and he intends to satisfy them. Desire is wrong, however, when it is contrary to the facts and thus prostitutes the mind, subjecting it to a rationalizing process, so that it must justify the facts in terms of that aroused desire. That is what is wrong.

Tempted Like Eve

See this in the Lord Jesus Christ. He, too, went through a time of temptation. He experienced the same order of attack that Eve did—not in the garden this time, but in a wilderness, in a barren place removed from all the comfort, luxury, ease, and pleasantness of a garden. There in the barren wilderness, after forty days of fasting, he was tempted like Eve.

The first temptation came on the same level as it did to her. She was tempted with regard to food, and the Tempter also came to the Lord and said to him, "If you are the son of God, turn these stones into bread. You need bread. After forty days and nights your body is crying out for bread. Surely God wants you to have bread; therefore turn these stones into bread." But Jesus' answer was, "It is written, 'Man shall not live by bread alone'" (Matt. 4:4). That is, bread is not the most important thing in life—God's will is. If you try to use bread for spiritual satisfaction, you are distorting God's design for man. That is not the purpose of bread. It is better to starve to death than to use it for a purpose God did not intend. So Jesus used the facts of the situation, the way God made man, and rejected the enemy's appeal, saying, "It's not right, and I won't do it."

Then the enemy took him to a high mountain and showed him all the kingdoms of the world, in all their pomp, glory, and majesty. This dream has entranced men for centuries. Some have caught a vision of even part of the kingdoms of the world and have fallen in love with the glory of it. But Jesus was shown all the kingdoms of the world in their alluring glory, with the suggestion that if he would fall down and worship the enemy he could have all this. This was clearly a delight to the eyes, something to titillate the senses and give a feeling of power. But our Lord rejected it because it was not in accordance with the facts. The facts are that man is made to worship God and God alone.

Then, you remember, the Devil took him up to the Temple and suggested he cast himself off in order to display the power he had. When the people saw that he could do this without physical damage, they would acclaim him as a divine being and he would gain popular appeal, the pride of life. Again he rejected it on the basis of the facts. He said, "No, it is written, 'You shall not tempt the Lord your God'" (Matt. 4:7). "God is in charge of life, and I will not allow anything to enrich me but what comes through his hands." Thus he rejected the temptation.

At this point it is important to note that Eve had not

yet sinned. Even though her desire is aroused and her mind has justified it, still it would be possible for her to recover herself, though very difficult. But, as James tells us, desire when it conceives gives birth to sin. And at this point it is recorded that when she saw that it was desired to make one wise, "she took of its fruit and ate." She acted on a lie and thus fell into the sin of becoming her own god, of making up her own rules, in violation of her humanity.

Darkness Begins

But there was still hope for the race. Adam had not yet fallen, only Eve. It is not in Eve that the race fell, it is in Adam that the responsibility ultimately lies. A battle has been lost, but not the war, yet. But then we read that after she took of the fruit and ate, "she also gave some to her husband, and he ate."

The ease with which Adam fell is dreadfully hard on the male ego. Think of it. Here is this whole account of the struggle of the Tempter to reach through to Eve, and only one little line about Adam, "she gave to him, and he ate." Yet in those innocent but ominous words, "and he ate," begins the darkness of a fallen humanity. The fatal twist now appears as mankind is transformed by this psychedelic drug (the forbidden fruit), and all men become the victim of a reverse psychology, mastered by emotional urges, no longer rational beings.

What is the value of this account for us today? The answer is that in this story we can see that what Jesus says of the race is true: it is the victim of a distortion which it is helpless by itself to remedy. We cannot change our basic natures. The fall has rendered us victims of emotional urges, and no matter how desperately we try to be rational about things, we cannot see the facts rightly. We do not even see the whole range of facts, and ultimately we find ourselves the unconscious victim of emotional twisting.

If anything points up the absolute necessity for the new birth, it is this. As Jesus said, there is no other way out for humanity except through him. "I am the way, and the truth, and the life; no one comes to the Father, but by me" (John 14:6). There is no way to see reality apart from Jesus Christ. It is he who opens the eyes, it is he who restores balance to life, it is he who redeems my humanity and helps make it possible for me to distinguish between what is right and what is wrong.

How do we know which is right, among the welter of voices that call to us today from every side, unless we judge them all by the voice of Jesus Christ? How can we find our way through the swamps of relativism that stretch out on every side, unless we are listening to the voice of the one who loved us and gave himself for us, that he might redeem us by destroying the works of the Devil?

> *Our Father, we pray that we might see once again, plainly and clearly, that there is no hope for us apart from the Lord Jesus and our following of him, trusting his love, and yielding ourselves to his redeeming grace. We pray that any who have not begun with him may begin by saying to him now, "Lord Jesus, save me. Come into my heart and life and begin your redemptive work with me. Make me different. Deliver me from the distortions of a fallen nature and grant that I, too, can see*

things as they really are." For those of us,
Lord, who have already begun, grant that we
may now resolve anew to follow him, to obey
him, to trust him, to day by day listen to what
he says. We ask in his name, Amen.

6 / The Package Deal

The evil act has finally been accomplished in the garden of Eden. We read, "she took of its fruit and ate; and she also gave some to her husband, and he ate" (Gen. 3:6). When desire, conceived and rationalized, issues at last in its ultimate form, it becomes an act or a settled attitude of the heart.

Now we come to stage three in the process of temptation. The Apostle James describes it this way: "Sin when it is full-grown brings forth death" (Jas. 1:15). Remember that God had said to Adam and Eve in the very beginning, concerning the forbidden fruit, "in the day that you eat of it you shall die" (Gen. 2:17). But the Tempter had said to Eve, "You will not die." He openly and defiantly challenged God's pronouncement. He said, "your eyes will be opened, and you will be like God . . ." (Gen. 3:5).

The way he said this made it sound like something glorious, exciting, and adventurous. He was saying to them by implication, "When you eat of this fruit you need no longer depend on this old Lord of creation; you will be lords in your own right. You can make decisions like God does, and do what you want to do." This has been the subtle lie that has hung over the whole human race from that day to this. But now the deed has been done, and we come to the moment of truth. Which view is right? Will they die? Is the Devil right?

> Then the eyes of both were opened, and they knew that they were naked; and they sewed fig leaves together and made themselves aprons (Gen. 3:7).

At first it is the Devil who seems to be right. He said they would not die, and when they took of the fruit they did not drop dead. He said their eyes would be opened and it is true that new knowledge was immediately granted to them. They saw things they had not seen before. Does that mean then that the Devil was right? No, because from the moment they ate they began to die—exactly as God had said. In Romans, Paul writes, "As sin came into the world through one man and death through sin, and so death spread to all men . . ." (Rom. 5:12). This was the moment at which that occurred.

Signs of Death

In this passage we will discover the signs of death. Death is not simply the moment when the breath leaves your body and you become a corpse. That is not death in its totality; that is simply the end of death. It is the end of a process which has been going on for some time, the beginning of which was so subtle that perhaps you did not even recognize it. It is the *beginning* of death which is traced in this Genesis account. The four things which are revealed here as marking the beginning of death are found in every person in the world, without exception. These things are present in the whole human race.

We all know that when we yield to temptation we experience pleasure. But what this account forces us to face is that with the pleasure comes an undesirable accompaniment, a fall-out of sin, which we cannot escape. It is a package deal. If we choose to take that momentary pleasure, we cannot choose to evade the accompaniment that comes—death.

The first mark of the beginning of death is this: "they knew that they were naked." Now they were naked all along. God did not make Adam and Eve with clothes on, any more than he makes human beings with clothes on today. We come into this world naked. They too came into the world naked, but they did not know they were naked until the Fall. Why not? Because they had never looked at themselves! Their interest was not in this direction. They were self-less.

Before the Fall they were concerned about the animals, and about the garden, and the work that had been assigned to them there. They were concerned with each other. But now suddenly they saw themselves. This awareness of nakedness is symbolic of the birth of self-consciousness. They saw themselves and the immediate effect was to bring shame and embarrassment upon them.

Test this in your own life. Is this not your most serious trouble, the fact that you are conscious of yourself? Is this not where you struggle the most? We all know that when we can forget ourselves, we do fine. We can speak, we can act, we can do many things well. But then the sense of self comes flooding back over us, and we begin to fumble, to stammer, to blush; suddenly we are all thumbs and left feet. Why? This is the effect of self-consciousness. But God did not make man that way. Man was never made to be conscious of himself. His interests were to lie outside himself; he was to be self-less.

Self-consciousness dogs every one of us every day, and the amazing thing is that to this very day we discover that clothing helps us. Adam and Eve, when they discovered they were naked, immediately made rough clothing out of fig leaves. They made themselves aprons and covered themselves. Here is the explanation for the fact that we find it psychologically necessary to clothe ourselves. In mankind's fellowship and intercourse with one another, clothing helps. It helps to make us feel more secure, more adequate, more able to face life. This is why women, when they get blue or discouraged, find it very uplifting to buy a new dress. One lady said, "Whenever I get down in the dumps I get a new hat." Her husband replied, "I wondered where you got them." So, like Adam and Eve, we reflect the same thing; we find ourselves making clothes to cover our self-consciousness.

We find this true at the psychological level as well. This is what lies behind the universal practice of creating an impression, projecting an image of ourselves. That is a form of psychological clothing. Physically, clothing is a way of changing our appearance so that we look different than we actually are. So it is with the matter of projecting an image. It is a way of trying to get people to think of us as different than we really are. This is why, at one time or another, we all find ourselves struggling with the matter of being honest, or being open. We find it difficult to be so. We do not want people to see us or think of us as we are. That is why we avoid close contact with one another. We do not want to spend much time with any one person because we are afraid he will see us as we are. You can see how this idea has simply permeated the human race ever since the moment self-consciousness was born in an act of disobedience.

The Hiding Instinct

The second mark that is present among us because of the disobedience of man, is the tendency to hide:

> And they heard the sound of the Lord God walking in the garden in the cool of the day, and the man and his wife hid themselves from the presence of the Lord God among the trees of the garden (Gen. 3:8).

Hiding is an instinctive reaction to guilt, and reveals the fact of guilt. When one of my daughters was a baby she had the habit of sucking her thumb. It carried over into late babyhood and we tried to help her with this. She began to feel very guilty about sucking her thumb and often, when we would catch her doing so, she would take it out of her mouth and hide it under her dress. Now, who taught her to do that? No one. No one needs to teach us such things; these are instinctive reactions. She hid because she felt guilty.

Here, then, is the first description of a human conscience beginning to function; that inner torment we are all familiar with which cannot be turned off no matter how hard we try. In fact, often the harder we try to ignore it the deeper it pierces and the more obdurate it becomes. Psychologists agree that guilt is a universal reaction to life, that without apparent reason or explanation all of us, without exception, suffer from guilt. This sense of guilt haunts us, follows us, makes us afraid. We are afraid of the unknown, of the future, of the unseen, just as Adam and Eve discovered themselves to be.

> But the Lord God called to the man, and said to him, "Where are you?" And he said, "I heard the sound of thee in the garden, and I was afraid, because I was naked; and I hid myself" (Gen. 3:9,10).

That is the heritage of the Fall, this sense of guilt. It is death at work in human life. But there is still a third aspect of this death:

> He said, "Who told you that you were naked? Have you eaten of the tree of which I commanded you not to eat?" The man said, "The woman whom thou gavest to be with me, she gave me fruit of the tree, and I ate." Then the Lord God said to the woman, "What is this that you have done?" The woman said, "The serpent beguiled me, and I ate" (Gen. 3:11–13).

There is much in these verses which I will pass by for the moment, to return to later. First I want to focus on the oldest game in the world, the favorite indoor sport of the whole race—passing the buck. The Lord said to them, "What is this that you have done?" And Adam said, "Well, the woman that you gave to me, *she* gave me the fruit, and I ate. It's her fault." The woman said, "Well, it's not my fault, it's the serpent's fault. The serpent beguiled me, and I ate."

Who Do You Blame?

This is the first human attempt to deal with the problem of guilt. Interestingly enough, it is exactly the same way by which we also try to relieve guilt. See how these factors are all related. It is self-consciousness which is the basic, fundamental, wrongness about human life. That is what produces guilt. Our awareness of self makes us ashamed, embarrassed, and guilty. Then in order to evade this sense of guilt, we do what Adam did. We say, "Well, it's not my fault. I'm but a victim of circumstance." He took it, you see, like a man: he blamed it on his wife. And she passed it along to the serpent.

But behind both excuses is the unspoken suggestion, very clear in this account, *that it is really God's fault* "The woman whom *thou* gavest me . . ." says Adam. If you had never given me this woman I would never have fallen into this sin. The woman immediately passes it on and says, "It is because you allowed the serpent to come into this garden, that's the trouble." Both are pointing the finger ultimately at God and saying, "It's all your fault."

That attitude pervades society and the whole of history. It is what I find married couples saying to one another all the time. The predominant problem in solving the tangles of a marriage relationship is to get the two to stop blaming each other. That is the hardest thing to do. But if they do it, the battle is two-thirds won. This is also the primary cause of racial strife. Each race is pointing a finger at the other and saying, "It's your fault!" This is what nations are doing in the international scene. We find ourselves universally yielding to this tendency to blame another and thus, ultimately, to blame God. Of course, we do not say *that*. Very seldom do you find a man coming out openly, outrightly, and blatantly saying; it is God's fault. But that is what lies beneath the surface; we are blaming God for the whole thing, trying to turn guilt into fate and to make of ourselves mere innocent victims, suffering from a breakdown in creation for which God is responsible.

The fourth result which this account reveals is found in verse sixteen:

> To the woman he said, "I will greatly multiply your pain in childbearing; in pain you shall bring forth children . . ."

And verse nineteen; to Adam he said,

> "In the sweat of your face you shall eat bread till you return to the ground, for out of it you were taken; you are dust, and to dust you shall return."

Pain, sweat, and death. Here are the limits of life. These are the prison walls that hem us in and mock all our hunger and yearning after freedom and fullness. Is it not clear that the whole race suffers from a sense of loss, a sense of limitation? Each one of us knows this feeling. We know there is more to life than we are experiencing—and how we crave it. How we long to find it, somehow, someway.

We pore over travel folders. We read about new opportunities for work. We join a club, or seek a new relationship with other people. We adopt a hobby. We try desperately to find some way to enter into the fullness which we feel life ought to present to us. We know it is there, but we have lost the way to it. Every effort we make, every step we take, every channel we follow, finds us flung back by these three things: pain; hard, grinding toil; and the black wall of death.

Why is it that we all have a sense of urgency about our work? Why are we forever saying, let's make the years count, let's use time to the full? Why do we use calendars and clocks? It is because we realize that we must die. Our time is limited. We are surrounded by walls we cannot break through. Every effort we make, if pressed too far, results in pain, struggle, and death.

That is what happened when the eyes of Adam and Eve were opened. They were indeed opened, but this is what they saw. They learned the hard, cruel facts of life lived apart from dependence upon God. They immediately knew a sense of self-consciousness, an awareness of guilt, an urge to blame the other, and that terrible, empty, hollow feeling of limitation, a sense of loss. What a cruel and dreary world these factors have produced. They are what the Bible calls "the works of the devil," works which he is free to accomplish because man has given him opportunity in the disobedient act of his heart.

The Second Adam

Well, we cannot leave the story there. We must remember that if there was a first Adam, from whose misdeed we all suffer, the good news is that there is also a second Adam, a man who came to reverse the works of the Devil, to free us, to loose us from their evil control. What does Jesus Christ do about these things?

What does he do about my self-consciousness? What does he do about this sense that I must depend upon myself? How does he change the accompanying guilt, embarrassment, and sense of inadequacy that immediately flood me when I realize that I must reckon on myself to meet the demands of life, but I do not have what it takes? What does he do? He turns my eyes from myself to himself. I learn to say with Paul, "I have been crucified with Christ; it is no longer I" but him (Gal. 2:20). He lives in me and whatever I do is done not out of dependence on myself but it is Jesus at work in me—and he is the adequate one. Just as soon as I believe and act upon that, I lose my self-consciousness. I become self-less. There is manifest in my life the outgoing givingness of the self-less Christ. Any moment I am doing that, that will be the nature of the life I live. That will be the nature of the life that you live in Christ. He completely destroys that tormenting self-consciousness which creates the embarrassment of life.

Well then, what does he do about my guilt? Ah, here is a glorious word! He comes to me when I stumble, when I fail or falter, when I find myself doing what I don't want to do and loathing myself because of it, and he says to me, "If any man be in Christ *there is no condemnation*. You don't need to worry, I know that you will do these things. I know that you have given way, and that you will give way; I know this. I know that you don't easily choose good and repudiate evil. I know that—but I love you and have died in your place. If you will look at this wrong thing and simply regard it honestly, as it is, immediately there is no condemnation. You are as loved as you ever were, you are as much mine as you ever were. Don't look back at the past, start right here, now, and let's go on."

What does he do about my urge to blame another person? He helps me greatly at that point. Jesus says to me, "Look, I'll give you the formula by which you can work out the problems of your life with other people. First, remove the beam that is in your own eye, then you'll see clearly how to help the other." When, in my relationship with another, I see what he is doing wrong but I don't know how to help him stop it, then I know that I am failing to remove first the beam that is in my own eye. I'm not following Jesus' directions.

But if I will; if I sit down and say, "What is it I am doing that makes him (or her) act that way to me, what is it *I* am doing?" then the situation wonderfully changes and I find that everyone begins to act differently to me, the whole world is different. The problem was not with others, it was with me. This is what Jesus helps me see. Openly, honestly, forthrightly, he tells me where the problem is.

What does he do about my fear of pain and sweat and death? You know what he does, don't you? He does not remove you from these things. In fact, you will often find yourself more frequently in them as a believer than perhaps you were before. The pain is still there, the need for toil is still there. And I know—you know— that there will come a time when we must face the fact of death. I won't be here always. I cannot carry on my work forever. I, too, must come to the place where I fold my hands and my spirit leaves this body and I am dead. What does Jesus do about this?

The Doorway

In each circumstance he goes with me into it, and I discover that what was to me a grievous cross, where something within me is put to death and which I fear, becomes a doorway into a new and greater experience than I could ever have dreamed. It is the old story of the cross and the resurrection. You can never experience the glory of a resurrection unless you have first experienced the death of a cross. Pain is transmuted into something different, a quiet peace which, though the pain is still there, makes it all worthwhile.

Like you, I look back on the painful experiences of my life and say, Those were the hours when I learned my greatest lessons. Those were the times when God spoke to me as at no other time—thank God for them. Then I can look at the demands of life for labor, sweat, and toil and know that those are the moments, too, when I find myself the happiest, engaged in that which produces a great sense of gladness, peace, and joy. And at last when I cross the river of death, it is only an incident. I know it will be so. It is but an incident, a momentary flash, and then all the greatness of God's glorious promise will begin to unfold in its shining actuality. "O death, where is thy victory? O death, where is thy sting?" (1 Cor. 15:55).

That is why Jesus Christ came. He finds us as people, human beings, involved in the nitty-gritty, hurly-burly of life, the struggle, the heartache, the grief, the sweat, blood, and tears of life, and he transmutes those things into patience and peace and joy. Christianity is not something to be experienced only in a religious service on Sunday—that's merely the whipped cream on top—but the wonderful body of it is mingled with the flow and flood of life itself. That is what makes it all so glorious. Jesus reverses the Devil's activity; he releases us from the works of the Devil.

What happens when, as Christians, we choose the wrong? Well, we experience death. This is inevitable.

"To set the mind on the flesh is death" (Rom. 8:6),
says the Apostle Paul. If we deliberately choose to dis-
obey our Lord we will experience the fourfold death
that follows inevitably in the great package deal of life.
It is the law of inevitable consequences which Paul describes so clearly when he says, "Whatever a man sows,
that he will also reap" (Gal. 6:7). But the glory of the
gospel is that the other side is true, as well. If you "sow
to the Spirit [you] will from the Spirit reap eternal life"
—and life as you have never known it before.

If you sow to the Spirit; if you obey and walk in fellowship with the Son of God, then in this life there
comes the sure reversing of all these evil things we have
been looking at and in their place will be the fellowship,
the joy, the glory, and the riches which are in Jesus
Christ. May God help us to cease our disobedience, to
stop challenging the authority of the Word of God, to
cease our apathetic lethargy that refuses to venture on
the facts that Jesus Christ reveals to us.

*Father, help us to understand ourselves and
to understand how clearly and relevantly these
words speak to our lives and our situation.
Grant to us, Lord, the courage to begin right
where we are—now. In Jesus' name, Amen.*

7 / God at Work

We now come to the same passage we discussed in the last chapter, but to look this time not at man but at God. For centuries a dirty lie about God has been making the rounds. This lie suggests that at the fall of man God ruthlessly lowered the boom on guilty Adam and Eve, that he gave them no chance to explain but simply tracked them down, sternly rebuked them (my children would say he yelled at them), began cursing everything in sight, and ended by booting Adam and Eve out of the garden—slamming and locking the door behind them. Nothing could be further from the truth! We must trace very carefully the actions of God in this account because, of course, this is the same way God will treat us after we fall into temptation.

God begins his dealings with man by raising three questions. The first one is found in verses eight and nine:

> And they heard the sound of the Lord God walking in the garden in the cool of the day, and the man and his wife hid themselves from the presence of the Lord God among the trees of the garden. But the Lord God called

to the man, and said to him, "Where are you?"
(Gen. 3:8,9).

It is most striking to me that all religions, apart from Christianity, begin with man seeking after God. Only the Bible starts with the view of God seeking after man. That highlights an essential difference between our Christian faith and the other great religions of the world. Furthermore, this first question in the Old Testament is matched by the first question asked in the New Testament. Here, God is asking man, "Where are you?" and in the New Testament, in Matthew, the first question that appears is that of certain wise men who come asking, "Where is he?"

If we take this account in the garden literally (as I believe we must), then it is clear that God habitually appeared to Adam in some visible form, for now Adam and Eve in their guilt and awareness of nakedness hide from God when they hear the sound of his footsteps in the garden. This indicates a customary action on God's part. He came in the cool of the day, not because that was more pleasant for him but because it was more pleasant for man.

We know from Scripture that whenever God appears visibly in some manifestation it is always the second Person of the Godhead, the Son, who thus appears. If that is true then we have here what is called a theophany, that is, a visible manifestation of God before the incarnation. Thus the One here who asks of Adam and Eve, "Where are you?" is the same One of whom later men would ask, "Where is he who was born King of the Jews?"

Now notice the importance of this question, "Where

are you?" Suppose you were on your way to a friend's house, but got lost and called him up to direct you. What would have to be his first question? "Where are you?" He would have to know where you are in order to have a starting point for his directions.

Today we are seeking to find a way out of the confusing situation which prevails in our world. We will never do it until we start with this question which God first asked man, "Where are you?" "Where am I?" Perhaps the reason many are unable to be helped today is either because they cannot or will not answer that question. Ask it of yourself now. Where are you? In the course of your life, from birth to death, moving (as you hope you are moving), to develop stability of character, trustworthiness, integrity of being, all these qualities which we admire in others and want in ourselves—where are you? How far have you come? Until you can answer that, in some sense at least, there is no possibility of helping you. What do you say?

Perhaps you will have to say, "I don't know where I am. I don't know. I only know that I am not where I ought to be, nor where I want to be. That's all I can say." If that is all you can say, at least it's an honest answer and therefore the most helpful answer you can give, and in that sense is the only right answer. "I don't know. I only know that I'm not where I ought to be."

Now God's second question to man is even more significant:

> And he [Adam] said, "I heard the sound of thee in the garden, and I was afraid, because I was naked; and I hid myself." He [God] said, "Who told you that you were naked?" (Gen. 3:10).

Let us be sure we read that question rightly. God is not asking Adam, "Look, who let the cat out of the bag about this? What rascal has been telling you tales out of school?" No, this is a rhetorical question. God does not expect a direct answer; it is a question designed to make Adam think.

An Inner Change

God is asking "How do you know this? You say you're naked; you didn't know that before. From what source has this knowledge come? Something has happened, a change has occurred; where did your knowledge come from?" The answer, of course, is that no one told him. Then how did he know?

It did not come from without at all, it came from within. A change had occurred within him and instinctively he senses that change and knows something that he did not know before. An evil knowledge has come to man, just as God said it would. The tree of which he partook was the tree of "the knowledge of good and evil," and by partaking man immediately gained an evil knowledge. From where did it come? From within. It is the birth of conscience, that strange faculty within us that tells us often what we do not want to hear. This is what God awakens Adam to see.

Now, in order to sense the full significance of this, we must link it with the first question, "Where are you?" which had only one proper answer; "I'm not where I want to be. I'm lost, hopelessly lost, hidden. I don't know where I am." Well, why don't you? Why is it that we have such difficulty pinpointing ourselves in our progress and relationship to the world around us? It is because of something within, isn't it? Remember Jesus said that it is not what enters a man which defiles him, but what comes from within. For out of the heart of man proceeds evil thoughts, fornication, murder, adultery, covetousness, licentiousness, pride, foolishness—all these evil things come from within and defile a man (Matt. 15:11–19).

It is what I am within which makes me ashamed and guilty, and sends me scrambling for fig leaves to cover myself up. Someone has well said, "If the best of men had his innermost thoughts written on his forehead, he'd never take his hat off." We know this is true. The basic, fundamental issue of humanity is not what is happening outside, but what is happening inside, within us.

Now God moves to his third question and it is in two parts, one addressed to the man and one to the woman.

> "Have you eaten of the tree of which I commanded you not to eat?" The man said, "The woman whom thou gavest to be with me, she gave me fruit of the tree, and I ate." Then the Lord God said to the woman "What is this that you have done?" The woman said, "The serpent beguiled me, and I ate" (Gen. 3:11–13).

Now there is something very interesting here. God asks them both the same question. He is saying to each, "Tell me, what is it that you did? Specifically, definitely, clearly; what is it that you did?" But there is an exquisite touch of delicacy and grace here which I hope you do not miss. He does not put the question in the same form to each. To the man he is forthright and blunt. "Have you eaten of the tree of which I commanded you not to eat?"

But to the woman he puts the question much more softly and gently. Every married man knows that his wife does not like a direct question. A man may say to his wife, "Where did you buy this meat?" Her answer is not usually, "At Safeway," but perhaps, "What's wrong? Why do you ask?" or, "I bought it where I always buy it." If he says to her, "Have you seen so-and-so lately?" she says, "What's happened?" Or perhaps she says, "Well, I never get out to see anybody—you know that." Or, "Why would I want to talk to her, anyway?" It is comforting to me to realize how fully God understands women and to see him put the question to her very gently. He says, "Tell me in your own way now, what is this that you have done?"

In their answer it is significant that both of them come out at the same place. Each blames someone else (we now call this "human nature," it is so widespread, so universally true), but when they come to their final statement they both use exactly the same words, "and I ate."

Reduced to the Facts

This is where God wants to bring them. This is what the Bible calls "repentance." It is a candid statement of the facts with no attempt to evade them, color them, or clothe them in any other form. It is a simple, factual statement to which they are both reduced; "and I ate." This is the point God has been seeking to lead them to.

Do you see how these questions have followed a certain course? God has made them say, first, "We're not where we ought to be—we know that. We ought not to be hidden here in the garden. We ought not to be lost. We ought not to require a question like this, 'Where are you?' " Then God has made them see that it is because something has happened within them. They have seen that they are *where* they are because of *what* they are, and that it all happened because they disobeyed, because they ate the forbidden food, they sinned. God has led them gently, graciously and yet unerringly to the place where each of them, in his own way, has said, "Yes, Lord, I sinned; I ate."

That is as far as man can ever go in correcting evil. He can do no more. But this immediately provides the ground for God to act. This is where he constantly seeks to bring us. This is seen throughout the whole Bible, in the Old and New Testaments alike. When God is dealing with men he seeks to bring them to the place where they acknowledge what is wrong.

Remember Jesus' dealing with the woman of Samaria at the well? After they have been involved in a discourse about the meaning of the water, he awakened her curiosity and interest by offering her living water so that she would not have to come to the well to draw. He then forthrightly put the demand, "Go and call your husband."

That elicits from the woman the only answer she could honestly give. "I have no husband," she says. Then Jesus lays it right out before her. "That's true," he says, "you have no husband. You have had five husbands, and the man you are living with now is not your husband, in this you said truly." He commends her for speaking the truth and from that point on he moves to open her eyes to the character of the One who stands before her (John 4: 7–26) .

Now this is what God wants to do with us. He finds us in our failure, our estrangement, our guilt, our sense of nakedness and loss, and immediately he moves to bring us to repentance. We misunderstand his moving. We think he is dragging us before some tribunal in order to chastise us or to punish us, but he is not. He is simply trying to get us to face the facts as they are. That is what he does here with Adam and Eve. As John says, "If we confess our sins, he is faithful and just, and will forgive our sins and cleanse us from all unrighteousness" (1 John 1:9).

As soon as Adam and Eve say these magic words, "and I ate," there are no more questions from God. There is no more prodding or probing on his part. God begins now to speak to the serpent, to the woman, and to the man. What he says to the man and the woman is not punishment, as we will see shortly, but grace. How badly we have misread these passages in Genesis. And when he gets through, we read these wonderful words:

> And the Lord God made for Adam and for his wife garments of skins, and clothed them (Gen. 3:21).

Here is the beginning of animal sacrifices: God sheds blood in order to make clothing for Adam and Eve. He made them from the skins of animals and therefore those animal lives were sacrificed to clothe Adam and Eve. This is but a picture, as all animal sacrifices are but pictures—a kind of kindergarten of grace—to teach us the great truth that God eternally attempts to communicate to us as men and women. Ultimately it is God himself who bears eternally the pain, the hurt, the agony of our sins. As John the Baptist said, "Behold, the Lamb of God, who takes away [who is continually taking away] the sin of the world!" (John 1:29).

Orphan Lambs

Paul uses a wonderful phrase in Ephesians, "accepted in the beloved" (Eph. 1:6, KJV). When we have acknowledged our guilt, when we have acknowledged that what we have done is contrary to what God wants, and we stand before him without attempting to defend ourselves, but simply in honest acknowledgment of our own doing, then, Paul says, we are "accepted in the beloved."

There were many sheep farms in the area of Montana where I grew up. Spring was the season when the little lambs were born. But spring in Montana can be brutal; sleet storms can come whirling down out of the north, and snow can still be three or four feet deep on the prairies. Often there are long, protracted seasons of bitter cold during lambing season.

Of course, when the sheep must bear lambs in that kind of weather many of the lambs and ewes die. As a result, sheep farmers have many mothers whose newborn lambs have died, and many newborn lambs whose mothers have died. A simple way to solve the problem, it would seem, would be to take the lambs without mothers and give them to the mothers without lambs, but with sheep it is not that simple. If you take a little orphan lamb and put it in with a mother ewe, she will immediately go to it and sniff it all over, but then she will shake her head as though to say, Well, that's not our family odor, and she will butt it away, refusing to have anything to do with it.

But the sheep men have devised a means of solving this problem. They take the mother's own little dead lamb and skin it, and take the skin and tie it onto the orphan lamb. Then they put the little lamb with this ungainly skin flopping around—eight legs, two heads—in with the mother. She pays no attention at all to the way it looks, but she sniffs it all over again, and then she nods her head, all is well, and the lamb is allowed to nurse. What has happened? The orphan lamb has been accepted in the beloved one.

There came a time when God's Lamb lay dead on our behalf and God took us orphans—he does it all the time—and clothed us in his righteousness, his acceptability, his dearness and nearness to him, and thus we stand "accepted in the Beloved One," received in his place. That is where repentance brings us.

It Doesn't End Here

But repentance is not only for the beginning of the Christian life. It is the way you start as a Christian, true. You come to God, like Adam and Eve, and say, "Yes, Lord, I'm the one. I've been running from you, I've been hiding from you, I've been estranged from you. It's because of what I've done. No one else is to blame but me." Then immediately God says, "I've taken care of all that. My Lamb has died for you and you stand in his place, acceptable to me." That is the way you begin the Christian life.

But that is only the beginning. Repentance is the basis upon which the whole Christian life is built. We must be continually repenting of those areas where we fail or fall back upon a way of living which God has said is not right. I find that as a Christian I am repenting far more than I ever did before; about things I never dreamed of repenting of before, because I am learning more and more that the Christian life is lived on a totally different basis.

I find I must repent of my self-dependence, and so must you. "Without me," says the Lord Jesus, "you can do nothing." If you attempt to do anything apart from that sense of dependence upon him to work through you, you need to repent, to change your mind, to accept again the covering of God, the clothing of his grace, the cleansing of his love.

This can, and perhaps will, occur dozens of times a day until we learn at last, little by little, to walk in this way, to count on his working. He is ours, and all that he is belongs to us. This is standard operating procedure, not just emergency treatment.

Now that Adam and Eve are standing before God, having acknowledged their sin, having said the same thing about it that God said, having admitted that they did the thing God said was wrong, his whole relationship to them has changed and he is on their side, he is "for" them, as Paul tells us God is "for" us (Rom. 8:31). He has been this way all along but Adam and Eve could not enjoy it until they repented.

> *Our Father, we thank you that we can echo with the Apostle Paul these words, "If God be for us, who can be against us?" If his love is made available to us then nothing can separate us from the love of God which is in Jesus Christ our Lord. We pray that this may have meaning for us more and more, as we learn to repent of our self-dependence and to cling consciously and helplessly to the continual flow of grace and strength from our loving God. We ask in the name of Jesus Christ. Amen.*

8 / The Devil's Burden

When Adam and Eve acknowledged their guilt, God immediately became their defender. His first word is to the Tempter, and it is one of scorching judgment. This is exactly in line with the promise given us in the first letter of John. John says, "but if any one does sin, we have an advocate [a defender] with the Father, Jesus Christ the righteous . . ." (1 John 2:1). As long as we defend ourselves, his defense is of no avail to us, but when we are ready to stop defending ourselves, we have a perfectly adequate defender with the Father. It is this same glorious defense which is exhibited here in this scene: the Friend of sinners stood that faraway day in the garden of Eden.

Now the Lord God speaks to the Devil:

> The Lord God said to the serpent, "Because you have done this, cursed are you above all cattle, and above all wild animals; upon your belly you shall go, and dust you shall eat all the days of your life" (Gen. 3:14,15).

As we have seen, this is not a snake God is speaking to, but "a shining one." Thus these words addressed to the Tempter are not a reference to the fact that snakes go around on their bellies. True, they do that, but they do not literally eat dust, as the word here says. This is figurative language, the words depict and describe humiliation and utter degradation. To this day one of the most humiliating things that anyone can be forced to do is to lie on his belly in the dirt. It means pride has been brought low; he is humiliated, shamed. "To eat dirt" has entered into the language as an expression of humiliation.

Curse of Humiliation

Now these are most significant words to the Devil. There is a passage in Isaiah that most Bible scholars feel describes the fall of the Devil. He is called there Lucifer, the Day Star, Son of the Morning, the angel who was created first among all the angels of heaven. In the pride of his heart he began to say to himself, "I will be like the Most High, I will act like God" (Isaiah 14:12–20). He is clearly identifiable with the shining one who appears in the garden, for it is this same thing that he suggests to Eve. "If you eat of this fruit," he says, "you will be like the Most High, you will be like God, knowing good and evil."

As far as we can judge, the fall of Satan occurred a long time before this scene in the garden of Eden. But it seems strongly suggested here that when Satan fell there was an immediate result in his own person which transformed him into a being of malevolent hatred against God. Perhaps there was a time when repentance was possible, but it seems likely that at this period of the history of our planet the Devil had passed beyond that stage. Yet it is apparent that judgment had not yet been carried out upon him.

Here, the significant thing is that we have the divine announcement to the Devil of the ultimate judgment that would befall him. Here he learns, perhaps for the first time, that his judgment would occur on this planet —that here, where he had so successfully derailed humanity through its first parents, he was to be put under an eternal curse, and the nature of it is to be continual humiliation and repeated failure.

The next time you are watching a TV western and you hear the hero say, "All right, you snake, crawl out on yore belly!" or perhaps, "Jest give me a chance and I'll make him lick the dust!" you'll know that you are watching a Sunday school lesson in action! At least this incident may help us to understand why these westerns are so popular. They always have the same plot, they have the same basic characters, and they invariably have the same ending; why then do people love to watch them so much? Is it not because they dramatize the eternal battle of the ages, the unconscious struggle that goes on in each of us? We want the "good guys" to win because we believe what God has said here, that it is the Devil's due to end up always in humiliation and defeat.

"But" you say, "that may be true in westerns, but that's not true in life. In life it's not the good guys that win; it's the evil ones." In life you find ruthless power triumphing over good, while the good end up as victims of senseless tragedy. What about those six million Jews who died under Hitler? What about the Negroes, Mexicans and other people who have been persecuted, hounded, smashed and killed, in so many places in our world today? What about the looting and burning of villages in Vietnam? Is this an example of the Devil's ultimate humiliation? What about the rape and murder of women and children in so many hell-spots of the world? You say, "All this is evidence that the Devil's defeat is but a fairy tale. It occurs in fiction, but it doesn't work out in fact."

Yet the declaration of this passage is that it does occur in fact, it is true. It is the Devil's burden that he will always end up as the defeated one, the humiliated one, fallen on his belly in the dust, eating dirt. The problem is, we don't wait until the end of the story. We do on television, because it only lasts a half-hour; but in life we turn it off before it gets through. But look on and see how this account tells us exactly how God proposes to accomplish the Devil's humiliation.

> "I will put enmity between you and the
> woman, and between your seed and her seed;
> he shall bruise your head, and you shall bruise
> his heel" (Gen. 3:15).

This is surely one of the most remarkable verses in the Bible. It was called by the early church fathers "the Protevangelium," which means the first preaching of the gospel. It is the clearest promise, first appearing in the Bible, of the coming of a Redeemer. There are several unusual features about this remarkable verse which reveal the divine hand.

First, you notice that it predicts an unending enmity to exist between two classes of humanity. Here is the beginning of the two divisions of humanity into which the Bible consistently divides the race throughout its whole course. Its first manifestation is that of enmity between Eve and the serpent, between the Tempter and the woman. "I will put enmity between you and the woman," says God. This is certainly understandable.

We can see why Eve would detest this one who had betrayed her by his lies, and as the effects of the fall would become more and more evident in her own life she would feel a continuing abhorrence against this one who had so cleverly and ruthlessly led her astray.

On the other hand, the enemy would surely hate her because she was now the object of God's love and his hand of protection was around her. But also, you will note, it was not enmity only between the woman and the Devil but between his seed and her seed, that is, the Devil's seed, and the woman's seed.

Seed of a Woman

Now without a doubt we have here a most remarkable prophecy of the virgin birth of the Lord Jesus Christ. There are those today who tell us that the virgin birth is an unimportant doctrine, but it is one of the most essential doctrines concerning our Lord. This startling prophecy cannot be explained in any other terms than that it finds fulfillment in the virgin birth of the Lord Jesus.

This concept of the seed of the woman is unique. Nowhere else in the Bible do you find such an expression occurring. Everywhere else in Scripture descent is reckoned through the male line. It is the seed of the man that determines the line of descent and all the genealogies of the Bible trace the line of descent through the male. The father's name is given and when the mother's name is given it is only incidental, referring to the wife of so-and-so.

We continue this in most societies today. Even today families bear the man's name. When a couple gets married it is the woman who drops her name and takes her husband's name. The name of the ensuing family bears the man's name; it is the male's seed which is the line of descent. But here we are distinctly told that the one who is to bruise the serpent's head is the seed of the woman. Now in all of human history there is only one who can fulfill that condition, Jesus of Nazareth.

In the opening words of Matthew's Gospel, we are told that when Joseph found that Mary was with child, even before they had come together, honest man that he was, gentle man that he was, "he determined to put her aside privately." That was the kindest thing he could do, the most gracious way he could handle the situation, because he knew the child was not his. But an angel appeared to him to tell him that "that which is conceived in her is of the Holy Spirit" (Matt. 1:20). That passage is clearly part of the original Gospel of Matthew. Luke has a reference to the virgin birth as well. Thus in the Gospels it is firmly established that Jesus was born of a virgin—of a woman but not of a man—the seed of a woman.

So the seed is Christ. This most impressive prophecy looks across the centuries to the day when Jesus would be born of Mary in Bethlehem. This is confirmed by the masculine pronoun which follows the statement, "I will put enmity between you and the woman, and between your seed and her seed; *he* shall bruise your head. . . ." The fulfillment of this promise, the seed of the woman, would be a man, born only of a woman.

In Old Testament times they could not see what was involved in this, but now we know it meant the humble birth at Bethlehem, the silent years in Nazareth, the darkness of Gethsemane, the opposition of Jerusalem, the hatred of Judas and Pilate and Caiaphas and Annas, the blood and death of a cross—all that was the bruising of the heel. Then there came the bruising of the head of the serpent in the glory of the resurrection morning. This whole promise is clearly fulfilled in Jesus Christ.

Brother Abel

But it is not only Christ, for now we know that "the seed" was not only an individual, but a people, against whom the enmity of Satan would continue throughout the whole of the age, for the whole history of the race. Thus the seed is not only Jesus but all who are "in Christ" as well, both Old and New Testament believers. The division here between two classes is not along racial lines or physical lines (there is no physical paternity of the Devil) but it is along spiritual and moral lines.

In the next chapter we learn that Cain was the first of "the seed of the devil," but the Pharisees of Jesus' day were Cain's brothers, because Jesus said to them, "You are of your father the devil, and your will is to do your father's desires" (John 8:44). The Pharisees of our own day belong to the same classification or division. On the other hand, Abel, Cain's brother in the flesh, was the first of "the seed of the woman," redeemed humanity. You and I who trust in Jesus Christ today are the brothers and sisters of Abel, members of that divine family who have, by faith, become part of the seed which is Christ.

Paul undoubtedly refers to this verse in writing to the Christians in Rome; he says to them:

> For while your obedience is known to all, so
> that I rejoice over you, I would have you wise
> as to what is good and guileless as to what is

evil; then the God of peace will soon crush
Satan under your feet (Rom. 16:19,20).

There, you see, is the bruising of the serpent's head,
to be accomplished not only by Christ but for those that
are "in Christ." Again Paul unquestionably refers to this
passage in the very first verse of Timothy where he says:

[God] who saved us and called us with a holy
calling, not in virtue of our works but in virtue
of his own purpose and *the grace which he
gave us in Christ Jesus ages ago* . . . (2 Tim.
1:9).

The phrase "ages ago" is literally, "before the age-
times." Here he refers to a promise that God gave of life
which would come through an individual, and which
was given before men began to count time. This could
only refer to this promise in the garden of Eden of the
coming of a Redeemer who would be the seed of the
woman and the source of life to men. Paul uses a similar
phrase in the opening words of the letter to Titus. He
speaks of those who, "in hope of eternal life which God,
who never lies, *promised before the age-times* . . ."
(Titus 1:2).

The situation then is clear. All those who have come
into this race through the normal line of descent from
Adam, as the seed of Adam, were born into the control
of the Devil. But God is calling out a seed of promise.
Any who exercise faith in this promised One, whether
it be faith before he came or faith in him now, are "in
Christ" and are also the seed of the woman. Between
these two (the Devil's seed and the woman's seed) is
enmity—unending enmity.

Surely we who know Jesus Christ and are Christians

experience this enmity frequently. Scripture describes it as the flesh warring against the spirit—and who of us has not felt it? Perhaps even now you are sensing this unending struggle. We know what God wants of us, we are learning how to walk in the Spirit, and yet often we desire to walk in the flesh—and we do. Because of this unending enmity between these two, we are constantly exposed to attack and temptation.

It extends to individuals as well. Galatians speaks of those born of the flesh who persecute "the children of promise" (Gal. 4:28,29). We well know that the world hates the truth of God, and seeks to ridicule it and to stamp it out; the world bans the Bible and burns the saints.

Strange Twist of God

But then a remarkable thing happens—this is the great thrust of the passage. The Devil's burden is that his very victories become also his defeats. There is this strange twist by which God in his power and wisdom turns the Devil's victories into utter defeat. He succeeds in bruising Christ's heel, but that bruised heel is what finally crushes the serpent's head. You can see this clearly in the cross. It was the bruising of the cross that made possible the smashing triumph of the resurrection. You can see it also in the events of your own lives and in the events of world history.

Take the matter of the death of those six million Jews under Hitler. We can hardly contemplate such a hideous thing occurring in our world. Yet it was that event, ghastly as it was, that made possible the birth of the nation Israel and set the stage for the fulfillment of promises which had lain unanswered in the Scriptures for century after century. The attempt of the enemy to stamp out the people of God—this strange nation, marked out by God as peculiarly his own among the nations of the earth—was turned into defeat and is now used to establish them in the land of promise.

In a most remarkable way, the distortion of truth in the stupid rituals and empty ceremonies of the medieval church in Martin Luther's day prepared the hearts of Europe for the blazing glory of the Reformation. People were so disgusted by what they were seeing, their hearts were so empty, they were so fed-up with materialistic indulgences and external approaches to God, that they were simply crying out in desperation for a note of reality. When Martin Luther nailed the ninety-five theses to the door of the church at Wittenberg, he struck a spark that caught fire throughout the tinder of Europe—tinder prepared by the Devil. It was the Devil's efforts that made possible the blazing fires of the Reformation.

We look back thirty or forty years and long for the days when youth were content with getting an education, finding a job, making money, going to church every Sunday, and fulfilling the moral demands of life. We think "Oh, those were the good old days—before youth got so wild and rebellious and uncontrollable." But we are blind to the frequent hypocrisy of those days, to the empty materialism, to the blurring of human values that was so common and so widely accepted.

True, the Devil has used this rebelliousness to push youth into revolt, but that is not the whole story. The glorious fact is that because of the rebellion of young people today there is a growing spirit of honest searching after truth that will not be denied. Young people are fed-up with superficial answers, and they will have nothing to do with the shallow, empty, materialistic gas they have been fed by a previous generation, but they look desperately for reality.

Surely this is the greatest hour to talk to young people about Jesus Christ our nation has ever known. I remember those dark days of the Depression when the Christian cause was regarded with scorn in intellectual circles. You could hardly bear a Christian witness on campus without being labeled a militant fundamentalist and turning off everyone. But now the campuses are wide open to hear what Jesus Christ is saying to men. There has never been such a moment. And who set it up? The Devil did!

I always rejoice in that account in Philippians of Paul's arrest by the emperor Nero. Paul is in prison, chained day and night to a Roman guard. I never read that passage without having to laugh with joy at the skill God demonstrates in turning that situation to his own glory. And Paul catches it. He says, "what has happened to me has really served to advance the gospel" (Phil. 1:12). Well, what had happened? God had chosen the most wicked and monstrous emperor the Roman Empire ever knew—the wretch, Nero—and had appointed him to head the Committee for the Evangelization of the Roman Empire!

He set him to the task of searching out the Empire to find the finest young men of the land and bring them to Rome. Then, every so often, he was to pick out one of the best of these and chain him to the Apostle Paul for six hours. You can predict what the result would be. One by one these young men were coming to Christ— the finest young men of Rome. It is undoubtedly from this band that many of the young men came whose names are recorded in the New Testament. When Paul closes his letter to the Philippians he says, "All the saints greet you, *especially those of Caesar's household*" (Phil. 4:22).

Today as well, God is turning the tables on the Devil. Satan is overreaching himself today as he always does. It is his fate to end up as those villains used to do in the old western melodramas: having trapped their victims and thinking they're on the very verge of success, the hero arrives and saves the day, and the villain stomps off, muttering through his mustache, "Coises! Foiled again!"

You can see this principle in your own personal lives. Which of you has not had some experience similar to that of the Apostle Paul who had that nagging, wretched thorn in the flesh given to him, prodding him and probing him? How he hated it, and asked God to take it away. But God said, "No, I won't. My grace is sufficient for you." As Paul pondered that there came a realization of what God meant, and he writes it down for us. He says, "I see now that it was given to me by God. It was the 'messenger of Satan,' true, yet God allowed it to come and God permitted it to remain, so that I might be kept from becoming proud and thus no longer useful to God. It is this that humiliates me, humbles me, makes me depend upon God and not myself, and therefore," he says, "I will glory in my infirmities, for out of weakness I am made strong" (2 Cor. 12:7–10).

That is the Devil's burden. Do you know anything more encouraging than that? The God we serve is the kind who is continually taking the worst the Devil can do and turning it into glorious victory. You will find that principle running through the Bible, from Genesis to Revelation. This is Christianity, entirely different from the principles by which the world seeks to work out its problems. Perhaps it has been best expressed to us in the words of the poet, James Russell Lowell.

> Though the cause of evil prosper
> yet 'tis truth alone is strong.
> Truth forever on the scaffold.
> Wrong forever on the throne . . .

It does appear that way, doesn't it? It looks as though truth is pinned down, crucified, and wrong sits forever on the throne. Evil seems to rule, walking with unhampered tread across the lives and hearts of millions of people. Yet the poet is right; it is not the throne of evil that ultimately succeeds; it is the cross, the place of apparent despair and defeat, the place of poverty, emptiness, and nothingness.

> Yet that scaffold sways the future,
> and behind the dim unknown
> Standeth God amid the shadows,
> keeping watch above his own.

That is the Devil's burden. Be glad you're not on his side—or are you?

We pray, Father, that you will take the scales from our eyes that we might see life as you see it, that we might look at the events of our day, not from the puny viewpoint of the flesh, but rather from the viewpoint of these great and eternal visions which allow us to see things as they really are. Help us to remember, Father, that no approach of the enemy needs to succeed, that we are called to be victors in Jesus Christ. "Sin shall not have dominion over us, for we are not under law but under grace." Let those thundering words strike our shackles off and set us free. Lord Jesus, we pray in your name, Amen.

9 / Love's Disciplines

Pain, toil, subjection, and death are the inevitable consequences of human disobedience to God, as we have seen. They were in the beginning, they are yet today. These are what the Bible speaks of as "death," in its widest sense. When Paul says "the wages of sin is death" (Rom. 6:23), he is not talking about a corpse; he is talking about this kind of death, the sense of pain, sorrow, toil, and subjection.

It is true that engaging in sinful acts or thoughts yields a temporary pleasure. Indulgence in sin is ego-satisfying, but as we have already seen, it is all a package deal. We cannot omit the bad parts and take only the good. It all goes together and thereby contributes to the sense of loss familiar to all, a sense of emptiness within, the restlessness of our race.

In looking at God's word to Adam and Eve after the fall we must now give closer examination to these four factors of pain, subjection, toil, and death, to see what they involve and why they were given to the race. We greatly need to understand this, because to understand it properly is to change us from grumbling, complaining critics of life to grateful, thankful optimists, fulfilling

123

that definition of Christians which is so often quoted: "completely fearless, continually cheerful, and constantly in trouble."

Now let us listen to God speak to the woman:

> To the woman he said, "I will greatly multiply your pain in childbearing; in pain you shall bring forth children, yet your desire shall be for your husband, and he shall rule over you" (Gen. 3:16).

There is something very interesting here. God's approach to the woman is always different than to the man, and certainly different than to the serpent. Notice that he says to the serpent, "Because you have done this . . ." and also to Adam, "Because you have listened . . ." but to the woman he makes no such charge of responsibility. There are consequences in her life that follow sin, but it is significant that he does not charge her ultimately with being at fault. We will see why when we come to God's word to Adam.

In each of these cases, the serpent, the man, and the woman, there are two consequences that follow. The serpent was to experience continual humiliation and ultimate defeat. In the case of the woman the consequences are pain and subjection. These are factors arising out of her nature and we need to look more closely at them.

Bound to Her Children

First, there is the factor of pain. Undoubtedly this verse does refer to the pain and danger of childbirth which women alone can experience. No man knows what a woman goes through in the birth of a child, but every mother understands. But the word refers to more than mere physical pain; it is basically the Hebrew word for sorrow. In Hebrew there is no word for pain but sorrow is the word universally used. It comes from a root which means "to toil"; thus, heartbreaking toil. This is perhaps why there has come into our language a description of birth pains as "labor," toil of a heartbreaking variety. It is evident, in view of the way the whole context has been developed, that this means more than simply physical pain; it refers also to the heartbreak associated with having children.

This is woman's primary experience as a result of the fall, the heartbreak of rearing children. It means that a mother's sense of success or failure in life is related to her children. A threat to a child is pain to a mother's heart. Perhaps every mother feels more sharply than the father does any sense of danger to or failure in her children. Mothers' hearts are bound to their children. We know this from experience and it is in line with what this passage suggests. The mother becomes so involved in the life of her children that what they feel, she feels; if they fail, she feels the heartbreak of it particularly strongly.

All this helps to explain a very troublesome passage in the New Testament which has bothered many at times, found in Paul's first letter to Timothy:

> I permit no woman to teach or to have authority over men; she is to keep silent. For Adam was formed first, then Eve; and Adam was not deceived, but the woman was deceived and became a transgressor. Yet woman will be saved through bearing children, if she continues in faith and love and holiness, with modesty (1 Tim: 12–15).

You can immediately see how difficult the passage is; no wonder many have struggled with exactly what it means. We will need to correct a few things in the translation of it, but if we lay the corrected passage alongside the passage in Genesis three, we are immediately helped to an explanation.

In the first place when Paul speaks of the woman being "saved," it must be clearly understood that this has no reference to her being regenerated, or born again. It is not talking about the entrance into the Christian life. Women and men alike are saved in that sense on the same terms, by faith in Jesus Christ. In Christ "there is neither male nor female" (Gal. 3:28); all come on the same basis. What Paul is talking about here is how a woman finds fulfillment, the sense of satisfaction in life. You find the same use of this later in the letter, where the apostle says to Timothy:

> Take heed to yourself and to your teaching;
> hold to that, for by so doing you will save both
> yourself and your hearers (1 Tim. 4:16).

Obviously here he is not talking about redemption, in the sense of regeneration; he is talking about saving his life in terms of making it worthwhile, rendering it useful and purposeful. This is the sense in which it is used in the second chapter about women. Women will find their lives fulfilled through bearing children.

But then it is not "if she continues" but, as it is literally in the Greek, "if *they* (the children) continue in faith and love and holiness, with modesty." That is in exact accord with what we find in Genesis where it is suggested that a mother's heart is wrapped up with the life and career of her children. She lives in and by her children. The meaning of her life is revealed in them, and if they succeed, she has succeeded, but if they fail, she has failed. I think every mother here will understand fully what I mean.

But this is not all that is part of woman's experience as a result of the fall. We read further,

> ". . . yet your desire shall be for your husband, and he shall rule over you" (Gen. 3:16).

The phrase, "your desire" is interesting. It comes from the Hebrew word "leg" and means "to run after." Her desires run after her husband. This is not primarily a reference to passion but to the hunger for approval. It is speaking of the fact that a woman finds her fullest sense of satisfaction in gaining her husband's approval. No other person can approach his approval in its significance to her. There can be no substitute for it. Others can be pleased and happy with her, but if he is not, she is distressed. He can be happy with her, and she doesn't care a fig what others think about her. Her desire thus finds its fulfillment in her husband—she longs to be important to him.

Rivalry for Leadership

Now I want to point out that this desire is not in itself a consequence of sin. This relationship of woman to man was present before the fall as well. The headship of the man was a fact from the creation. It is the latter phrase of the sentence that marks the result of the fall, "he shall rule over you." If, in imagination, we can put ourselves back with Adam and Eve before the fall in that blissful scene in the garden of Eden, we can see that the relationship of the woman to the man consisted of a natural desire to follow. She came out of man and was made for him, to be his helper and to work toward his goals. It was a natural yielding to which she offered no resistance but found herself delighting in the experience of following the man.

But now, as a result of the fall, a perverse element enters into this. A struggle occurs, a tension ensues, in which the woman is torn between the natural God-given desire to yield to her husband, and at the same time, the awakened desire to exert her will against his, a perverse urge to rivalry or domination. This is what creates tension in women, as a result of the fall. It means that in order to exert proper leadership, men must sometimes do so against the will of their wives. This constitutes "ruling" in the sense intended here. The struggle and tension produced in women's lives creates the tyranny that sometimes ensues in marriage, where the man rules with an iron hand. This is never justified in Scripture. Husbands are exhorted to love their wives and to deal patiently and kindly with them, as the Lord Jesus does the church. But in fallen man it results in the tyranny of man over woman, often as a result of the struggle within her.

Perhaps a woman herself can describe this most accurately. These words, describing this very reaction, were written by a woman:

> Millions of words have been written on how a man should love a woman. I would like to give you my reflections on the things a man should not do in loving a woman. First, *don't yield your leadership*. That's the main thing. Don't hand us the reins. We would consider

this an abdication on your part. It would confuse us, it would alarm us, it would make us pull back.

Quicker than anything else it would fog the clear vision that made us love you in the first place. Oh, we will try to get you to give up your position as number one in the house—that's the terrible contradiction in us. We will seem to be fighting you to the last ditch for final authority on everything, for awhile, but in the obscure recesses of our hearts we want you to win. You have to win, for we aren't really made for leadership. It's a pose.

Coronet, February, 1955

Would you like to know who wrote that? Judy Garland! It is the story of her own experiences with men.

This is why a woman can never find happiness in marriage until she takes seriously the words of Scripture, Wives, be subject to your husbands, as to the Lord (Eph. 5:22).

One of the two major factors producing the terrible breakdown in marriage in our country today is this failure of women to understand this principle; that it is their privilege, under God, to find fulfillment in submission to their husband's leadership. They are not to resist it, or try to rival him in these matters.

I am continually amazed at how much this needs to be asserted these days, especially so among Christians. I heard recently of three Christian wives who raised the question in a discussion: If a woman feels the Lord wants her to do certain work at church or something else in connection with the Lord's work, and her husband doesn't want her to do it, what should she do? They decided that she should go ahead anyway and if the husband objected or raised a fuss, it could be interpreted as suffering for Christ's sake.

I don't think I could find a more classic example of repeating the pattern of temptation found here in Genesis. There is the same subtle desire for an ego-satisfying activity, coupled with a rationalization that, in effect, cancels out the Word of God, thus permitting an activity that is contrary to what God wants. It is God who said, "Wives be subject to your husbands as to the Lord. Therefore, he cannot be and is not pleased by wives who will not do so. No amount of justification on the ground of the nature of the work being done will cancel out that disobedience. It usually results from a subtle form of desire for domination.

I would like to give you in that connection another interesting quotation, this time from then Governor Mark Hatfield of Oregon who, in a very interesting article, tells how surprised reporters were, when they reported his marriage, that his wife had included the word "obey" in her marriage vows. He went on to discuss how he and his wife had come to the conviction that this word should be used and he says:

> I can recall the very evening that Antoinette first broached the subject. We had been invited to spend an evening at the home of married friends. Because we were considering marriage ourselves, perhaps we were sensitive to the relationship between this couple. At any rate, something about them puzzled us.

Then, driving home, we suddenly put our finger on it. The wife, and not the husband, had taken charge of the evening. "Charles, dear," she had said as we came through the door, "won't you take their coats to the bedroom?" And later, "The phone is ringing, Charles." And still later, "Charles, don't you think it's time for some refreshments?" And each time Charles jumped up from his chair and dutifully did her bidding.

Oddly, Charles is not a Mr. Milquetoast; he is an aggressive businessman with a reputation as a go-getter. Nor is his wife mannish or overtly bossy. They are normal, average, likable people. In fact, I think it was the normalcy of the situation that alarmed us. The wife was the head of that household and nobody, least of all Charles, saw anything wrong in it.

As I drove home that night, Antoinette suddenly said, "When I get married, I want a husband, not a partner." I looked at her in surprise. "What do you mean?" "Perhaps I mean that I don't think there can be a real partnership in marriage," she replied. "It's like this car. We're traveling along together going to the same place, but you're driving. Both of us can't drive. And I don't think there can be two drivers in a marriage, either. One person's got to be at the wheel, and when it's the woman, I don't like what it does to her. Or to him. But it hurts her most."

Those are wise words, reflecting exactly the position of Scripture in this matter.

Well, now, some of you women are saying, "What a raw deal we've been handed. Talk about cruel and unusual punishment, this is it." But is it? Is this intended to be punishment? This is a question I wish to face as we look at these verses, because these words are often interpreted as though all this is a punishment dealt out by God upon the race, and woman's lot is the heaviest of all. But it is not punishment and was never intended to be punishment. If you will wait until we can look together at Adam's word, you will see why.

> And to Adam he said, "Because you have listened to the voice of your wife, and have eaten of the tree of which I commanded you, 'You shall not eat of it,' cursed is the ground because of you; in toil you shall eat of it all the days of your life; thorns and thistles it shall bring forth to you; and you shall eat the plants of the field. In the sweat of your face you shall eat bread till you return to the ground, for out of it you were taken; you are dust, and to dust you shall return" (Gen. 3:17–19).

In these verses we learn for the first time the nature of the sin that caused the fall of the human race. It was not merely that Adam ate the fruit in disobedience to God. There was something before that, and God records it. "Because you have listened to the voice of your wife." That was the sin that began the fall of Adam and brought the misery of death upon the race.

Now there are times when the wisest thing a man can do is to listen to the voice of his wife. Many a woman gives excellent advice to her husband, and a man is foolish who does not pay attention to what his wife says. Surely Pontius Pilate would have saved himself grief if he had listened to the voice of his wife when she sent word to him, "Have nothing to do with that righteous man, for I have suffered much over him today in a dream" (Matt. 27:19). But he ignored the voice of his wife, which would have saved him.

Whatever You Say, Dear

But here Adam is charged with guilt because he listened to the voice of his wife—when it was different from the voice of God! That is the point. It was wrong for him to take his leadership from her. It was a denial of the headship which God had established. Paul gives us the order of headship when he says, "The head of every man is Christ, the head of a woman is her husband, and the head of Christ is God" (1 Cor. 11:3). It was also the Apostle Paul who tells us that Adam was not deceived in the fall. The woman was deceived. She was deluded, for she believed the enemy. She thought he meant it when he said they would become like God if they ate the fruit.

But Adam was not fooled. He knew that if they ate the fruit the fall would follow; that they would lose their relationship to God, and that death would occur. He knew it, but he deliberately disobeyed God and set his wife above God. He denied the headship of Christ over himself and surrendered his own headship over the woman.

This has been the major failure of man in marriage ever since, and the second major cause producing chaos in marriage today; a man who refuses to lead, a man who turns over to his wife the ultimate responsibility of the family. He views his sphere as that of making a living and gives to her the job of making a life. He refuses to make decisions, refuses to give direction or to show concern over the way the family is going, or to enter into the problems of child discipline and training. All this constitutes failure and the breakdown of the headship of man over woman and of God over man.

There are basically two false concepts in marriage which this highlights for us. One of them is that man, when he gets married, is to please his wife by doing whatever she wants to do. Usually this results in the chinless, spineless, supine, Caspar Milquetoast kind of individual. But it is a widespread approach to marriage today, and sociologists are telling us it is rapidly producing in our country a matriarchal society. When boys, raised at home, do not have a male image to relate to, they do not know what a father is supposed to be—they never see one—so they relate to their mother and the mother becomes the dominant factor in the family. This turns society upsidedown and produces much of the weakness, conflict, and violence we are seeing so widely today.

The second false concept in marriage is for the man, regarding himself as the head, to interpret this to mean he may do whatever he wants; that he is to run the home to suit himself and his pleasure is the determining factor in what occurs. He becomes a tyrant, a dictator. This is as wrong as the first view and equally contrary to the Word of God.

The truth is that he too is under authority. He is to submit to the headship of Jesus Christ. He is to follow him. If a man refuses to do that, then his home is bound to go on the rocks one way or another, either in internal conflict or in actual outward break-up. He is to follow the Lord Jesus Christ as he is revealed in the Word of God and by prayer. Man is to follow him whether he, or his wife, feels like it or not—that's the whole issue. He is kindly but firmly to insist that *they* are to do what God wants.

Toil and Death

Because Adam refused to do that and listened rather to the voice of his wife, letting her determine the course of the marriage, the fall resulted. Two things came from it; first, toil. The ground was cursed; thorns and thistles were to appear and cover the ground. This suggests an immediate lowering of fertility. Nature produces only in response to God's continuing manifestation of power. All God needs to do to change the course of nature is to reduce the flow of power to it and lower fertility results. Nature then goes out of balance and the result is an increase in strong plants, such as thorns and thistles. The presence of these, on a widespread scale, indicates that nature is out of balance. It is a reflection of the eccentricity which has come to man. Nature is out of balance because man is out of balance.

This is why we must struggle so to make a living. Man is reduced to unending toil and sorrow. It is interesting that the word *toil* is exactly the same word in Hebrew that is translated *pain* for the woman. It is heartbreaking sorrow, caused by labor and toil. This is the reason for the so-called "rat race" of life, why we are constantly under pressure to get more out of a reluctant nature.

Work is not the curse given to man; work is a blessing. It is toil that is the curse. If you do not have work to do, you are of all people most miserable. Work is a blessing from God; but hard, grinding, toiling work is the result of the fall.

Then the second factor which resulted from Adam's failure to observe his headship is death. God said, "In the sweat of your face you shall eat bread till you return to the ground, for out of it you were taken; you are dust, and to dust you shall return." It is this sense of death, lurking at the boundaries of life, which gives us the feeling of futility about life.

Remember what God said to the rich man who built barns, filled them up, and then said to himself, "Soul, take your ease, for you have all you need." God said to him that night, "Fool! This night your soul is required of you." Then he asked this question, "Then, whose will these things be?" (Luke 12:16–21). Yes, that is the question death forces us to face, isn't it? You struggle to amass property, all the good things of life. But what a sense of futility there is in having to pass them along to somebody else, someone who didn't turn a finger to gain them.

Years ago a young friend of mine said to another, "My uncle died a millionaire." The man replied, "He did not." The young man said, "What do you mean? You didn't know him, how do you know he didn't die a millionaire?" "Because," the man said, "no one dies a millionaire?" The young man said, "What do you mean?" And the older man simply asked, "Who has the million now?" No, we never die millionaires. Naked we came into the world and naked we will leave it. We have nothing that we can take with us; we must leave it all behind. We are dust, and to dust we will return.

Is It Punishment?

There is the sentence of God—pain, subjection, toil, and death. Now, is this punishment? I promised to face this question with you. Is it punishment? Is this the result of our folly for which we must grind our teeth and struggle all our life, a curse for what Adam did? No, it is not. It only appears to be punishment when we refuse it and resist it or rebel against it. But these things were never intended to be any kind of punishment.

They are instead intended to be helps to us, means by which we are reminded of truth. Their purpose is to counteract the subtle pride which the enemy has planted in our race which keeps us imagining all kinds of illusory things—that we are the captain of our fate and the master of our soul—these arrogant pretensions we constantly make, that we can solve all the basic problems of existence.

But we are constantly being reminded that these things are not true. Death, pain, toil and subjection are limits that we cannot escape. They are there to cancel out our egocentric dreams and reduce us to seeing ourselves as we really are. We are dust. We are but men. We are limited, dependent. We cannot go it alone—we desperately need other people, and we desperately need God. The hour of greatest hope in our lives is when our eyes are opened to this basic fact and we say, "Lord, I can't make it without you. I need you desperately." These are the things that remind us of that.

Who of us has not had a loved one suddenly pass away and in the presence of death we sensed that we were facing a stark fact which could not be explained away or covered up or shoved under the rug. There it was, facing us every time we turned around. It was to remind us of what we are, and where we are. You will find this principle running all through the Bible. Jacob limped upon his leg for the rest of his life after wrestling with the angel at the brook of Peniel. It was to remind him that he was a man, nothing but a man, dependent upon God. It was to turn him from reliance upon his own craftiness and the cleverness of his own wit. Moses was denied the right to enter into the land, because of his failure. It was a reminder to him, who had been given great prestige and power before God, that he was nothing but a man and that he could live only within the limitations of God.

A sword came upon David's house because of his sin. It was a reminder to him, constantly, that though he was the king he could not do his own will, or act as he pleased. He was a man, dependent upon God. Paul had a thorn in the flesh given to him, and he cried out against it. But God reminded him that it was given to him to keep him humble in order that he might be a useful instrument in God's hands, dependent upon his love and grace.

Remember the closing words of the Twenty-third Psalm? How many times we have quoted that Psalm!

> Surely goodness and mercy shall follow me
> all the days of my life; and I shall dwell in the
> house of the Lord for ever (Ps. 23:6).

Some quaint commentator has said that those two words, goodness and mercy, are God's sheep dogs. This is the Shepherd's Psalm. David wrote it when he was but a lad, keeping sheep. In referring to the goodness and mercy of God, he is referring to the sheep dogs that nip at the heels of the flock and keep them in line, driving them into place. "Surely goodness and mercy shall follow me all the days of my life," nipping at my heels, humiliating me, turning me back from that which looks good but is really evil, keeping me from getting what I think I need, and what I think I want. But in the end we must name these what God names them—goodness and mercy!

No, these things are not punishment. These are the disciplines of grace. They are what Paul refers to in Hebrews twelve. If you are not chastised, disciplined by God, you are not a child of his. These things are given to bring you into subjection, for God loves you, and he wants you to be what he made you to be—and what your own heart longs to attain. Your pride needs to be crushed, humiliated; your ego smashed; your dependence upon yourself broken; your reliance upon your abilities, your background, your education, pulled out from under you—until you lean upon the God who made you and who is able to supply all that you need. When you do that, you will discover that "whoever would save his life will lose it, and whoever loses his life for my sake will find it" (Matt. 16:25).

Lord, we pray that you will teach us to view all the sorrowful, painful, struggling times in our lives as you view them—as instruments of your grace, faithfully following us until we learn finally to depend always on you. Teach us to trust you, Father, in the name of Jesus, Amen.

10 / Exit from Eden

In order to understand this last scene, it will be helpful to review quickly what we have learned so far. We have looked at the process of temptation—the arousing of desire, the mind's rationalization of that desire, and thus the moving of the will to an act of disobedience. This is always and forever the process that temptation follows. Then we saw how the account immediately records the fact that death entered the scene.

What the Bible means by death is far more than simply the ending of life. In the sense this account reveals, death is first a very vivid feeling of self-consciousness. We are made immediately aware of ourselves, and this brings with it an accompaniment of shame, guilt, and fear. Along with that there is a sense of defensiveness, a desire to blame somebody else; and then a great sense of loss or limitation, an enslavement, follows. These were inevitable after Adam's sin, and they still are.

The next step is one of repentance. We have seen how God, in grace, skill, and tenderness, leads this guilty pair back along the path they have come, and helps them to see what they have done. Repentance consists of two things. First, the awareness of the course of

141

temptation; it comes from within. God helps Adam to see that his sin arose not from anything outside him but from something within. Second, the pair acknowledge the fact of their disobedience. They both come to the place where they say, "Yes, we ate."

Following their confession, God moves to give a promise of grace. There is the announcement of defeat for the Tempter, and his judgment is declared. Then certain helps are provided to the man and woman to keep them clinging in dependence upon God, which is the only place of safety, the only place of security and strength in life. These helps are pain, subjection, toil, and death.

Changed for Life

That brings us to the last three steps of the process traced in this chapter, and these three are extremely significant. What happens after God acts in grace to give a great promise and to set "sheep dogs" nipping at the heels of mankind to bring individuals into the place of blessing? The first thing is an act of faith on Adam's part:

> The man called his wife's name Eve, because she was the mother of all living (Gen. 3: 20).

In order to understand that we must link it immediately with verse fifteen where we have God's statement to the serpent about the woman:

> "I will put enmity between you and the woman, and between your seed and her seed; he shall bruise your head, and you shall bruise his heel."

That verse deals with the woman's issue, the seed of the woman. Verse twenty deals with the same. The woman is to become "the mother of all living." In response to this promise of a seed to come through the woman, Adam changes his wife's name. In the beginning, her name was not Eve (isn't it strange that we never refer to her as anything but Eve?) but Adam called her Ishsha which is the Hebrew for woman:

> Then the man said, "This at last is bone of
> my bones and flesh of my flesh; she shall be
> called Woman [Ishsha], because she was taken
> out of Man [Ish] (Gen. 2:23).

He called her Out of Man, and that was her original name. But now, because of God's promise, he changes her name to *Chavah*, which means "Life." Our English word *Eve* is simply an anglicization of this Hebrew word *Chavah*.

Ordinarily verse twenty is taken to indicate Adam's understanding that a race of men and women are to come from Eve; thus, she is to be the mother of all living. But that was rather obvious from the beginning. Adam and Eve knew that they were to be mother and father of a race, because God had told them to multiply and fill the earth. But this verse, you will notice, immediately follows the announcement that the ultimate doom of man is death. God has said to Adam, "You are dust, and to dust you shall return," and Adam understands from that that he is now to become the father of a doomed race; that because of his sin, that which he begets is doomed to death from the moment of birth.

How certainly we know the truth of this. We begin to die the moment we are born, and the process goes on until it results in the inevitable conclusion of the grave. I am always faintly amused by the optimistic reports of the medical profession about the present increase of life span, though I am sure this is progress and is something good. But there is always the implication that ultimately we are going to win this battle. Yet the interesting thing is that though we have won great victories in the medical field, the death rate has remained exactly what it has always been—a flat one hundred percent.

Adam realizes that this is true. But if you read carefully here you will notice something important: Adam changes the name of his wife because Eve has heard God's promise and believed it. This is the only possible explanation for verse twenty. When a human being, guilty in sin, believes the promise of God, truly believes it, he or she passes immediately from death into life. In recognition of that change, Adam calls his wife *Life*, because she has passed from death into life.

"Therefore," he says, "she is the mother of all living," that is, the first of a long line of those who would pass from death into life. This ties in exactly with the promise of the seed of the woman which would ultimately come and which would bruise the serpent's head. All those associated with Christ become part of this redeemed humanity, which is the seed of the woman, and Eve was the first of that line.

All this corresponds with the significance of a change of name throughout the rest of the Bible. Have you noticed how many biblical characters change their names, and always with this same significance. It means that a person has also changed his nature, changed his character. He has become a different person. A bit later in Genesis we learn that God changed the name of Abram to Abraham, and the name of Abram's wife, Sarai, to Sarah. These names are significant.

Later he changed the name of Jacob (which means a supplanter, a usurper) to Israel (which means a prince with God). It is always *God* who changes these names. In the New Testament our Lord changed the name of Simon, the brother of Andrew, to Peter, because he said he would become like a rock, which is what Peter means. He also changed other names. Saul of Tarsus becomes Paul, which means "little." He lost his conceit and became little in his own eyes and so his name was changed to Paul. Thus you have all through the Scriptures this significant change of name which refers to change in the whole nature of the person.

This is therefore not a promise that Eve was to become the mother of a race of literal human beings; this is the promise, rather, that she is to be the mother of those who would find life through Jesus Christ. Thus the immediate response to the promise of God is an act of faith on Adam's part. After all, this is the only proper response to a promise; to believe it and to act on it. And that is what Adam did.

Throughout the whole account in this chapter there are only two things that man can and does do, with regard to the problem of sin: he repents, and he believes. That is all. He exercises repentance and faith. Throughout the rest of the Bible, repentance and faith are the means by which the problem of human evil is handled: repentance, an acknowledgment of the facts; and faith, a laying hold of the promise of God by an act of the will. It is thus that man lays hold of God's grace.

Mark of Acceptance

Now the divine activity begins again:

> And the Lord God made for Adam and for
> his wife garments of skins, and clothed them
> (Gen. 3:21).

We have already noted the significance of this in part; this was a sign of God's redemptive activity. With the sacrifice of another life he clothed Adam and Eve. It is a beautiful picture of how we are clothed with the righteousness of Christ. We are given his standing before the Father.

But clothing is not required for God's benefit. It does not make any difference to God that Adam and Eve are naked. In fact, as Hebrews tells us, we are all always naked before God: everything is naked and open in his sight (Hebrews 4:13). It is not God who requires this clothing, nor is it Adam and Eve, though it may have bothered them to be naked before God in their fallen condition. But it is because of the others who would see them that they are clothed. Clothing is for *public* appearance. God desires that the mark of his acceptance and acknowledgment of them be manifest to the whole universe. That is why Adam and Eve are clothed, and this is the primary purpose of clothing.

We are concerned about clothing today, because it makes us acceptable in the eyes of others. We feel that we look better, and most others think so too. Remember that in the story of the prodigal son, in the New Testament, the first thing the father did when the son returned home was to clothe him with a new robe. It is a public mark of acceptance, a public demonstration that he was back in full favor with his father. Also, in the story of the healing of the demoniac of Gadara, we are told that the Lord cast many demons out of this man, a legion of devils. When the disciples returned to the Lord they found the former demoniac sitting at the feet of Jesus, "clothed and in his right mind" (Mark 5:15). That clothing is a significant expression of his return to normalcy.

The importance of clothing in its symbolic significance was underscored for me one day as I was driving down the street near where the youngsters were getting out of high school. I passed by three boys with hair down to their shoulders and rather grubby clothes on. Two of them were not so bad, but one of them was in a terrible state. His clothes were filthy, his hair was matted and dirty, and it was, I confess, revolting to me to look at him.

But it set me to thinking. What makes these youngsters dress this way? Why are they so fiercely determined about it? Why is it so important to them that they must defy authorities and customs and traditions in order to dress in this fashion? As I thought it over, I recalled this story of when man was clothed by God. I saw immediately that what lies behind the fierce desire of some young people to dress in these weird fashions is that clothing reflects the inner condition of the heart. We want our clothing to be expressive of what we are. The young people's dress is therefore an attempt, in some sense, to be honest.

When I thought of it that way I could see that perhaps we are superficial in our attempts to correct these conditions by outward legislation. If clothing does reflect an inner condition, it does not help much to force an outward change. Clothing means something. The proof of that is that whenever any of these young people (as I have seen happen several times now) become converted and their inner rebellion ceases, the first sign of it is that their clothing changes and often they get a haircut. Their whole outward look changes because the inward attitude has changed.

Now notice that *God* clothed Adam and Eve. He killed the animals, he made the skins, and he clothed them. They did not even clothe themselves, but he dressed them. It is important that we let God do this to us. Not long ago a young man came to me, burdened by a moral failure in his life. He was heavy with guilt and he talked it all out with me. Together we went through the Scriptures, but he said to me, "Yes, I know these things. I know that God has forgiven me, but I can't forgive myself. I feel unclean, and I can't look at myself as being anything but unclean."

Then I retold him the story of Peter on the housetop in Joppa, when he was waiting for an unknown delegation to come from Cornelius. God prepared him for that encounter by letting down a sheet from heaven, filled with unclean and clean animals, and said to him, "Rise, Peter, kill and eat." Peter protested and said, "No, Lord, I have never touched anything unclean in my life." But God immediately rebuked him, "Peter, don't you call unclean what I have called clean" (Acts 10:9–15).

I said to this young man, "Isn't this what God is saying to you? The Scripture says, 'If we confess our sins, he is faithful and just, and will forgive our sins and cleanse us from all unrighteousness' [1 John 1:9]. Now don't you dare to call unclean what God has cleansed.

That's an insult to God's grace." He immediately saw the point and was tremendously helped.

Thus, following the act of faith on Adam's part, there is the cleansing and public mark of acceptance by God, so that it is clearly demonstrated to every being in the universe that Adam and Eve are now received of God and owned again by him. Well, then, if that is the case, how shall we explain this last section which seems to be totally inconsistent.

> Then the Lord God said, "Behold, the man has become like one of us, knowing good and evil; and now, lest he put forth his hand and take also of the tree of life, and eat, and live for ever"—therefore the Lord God sent him forth from the garden of Eden, to till the ground from which he was taken. He drove out the man; and at the east of the garden of Eden he placed the cherubim, and a flaming sword which turned every way, to guard the way to the tree of life (Gen. 3:22–24).

God seems to have drastically changed his attitude, hasn't he? He had just accepted Adam and Eve, dressed in the new clothing which he himself had provided, but suddenly he banishes them from his presence, drives them out, slams and locks the door behind them, and sets a guard in the path to keep them from coming back in. Is there not something wrong here?

The Way to the Tree

If we read this passage that way, we have surely misread it. It is important that we note carefully exactly what it does say. Notice that verse twenty-two is one of the few unfinished sentences in the Bible. God acknowledges that man has fallen into a condition of self-centeredness. He says, "the man has now become like one of us." Man knows good and evil by relating it to himself. This is the basic problem with mankind. We have no right to know good and evil by relating it to ourselves, but that is what we do all the time.

It is recorded in the Book of Judges, "Every man did that which was right in his own eyes" (Judges 17:6). That is the formula for anarchy. It means we are relating and judging everything by the way it appears to us. This is the way God does it, for he is the measure of all things, but it is wrong for man. God acknowledges this condition and, having done so, he now faces the problem of the other tree in the garden.

This is not the tree of the knowledge of good and evil, now, but the tree of life. God says, "What if man, doomed now to guilt, shame, limitation and loss, should now reach forth his hand and take and eat of the tree of life, and live forever." It would mean that man would never physically die but would go on in his evil condition forever. Notice that God leaves the sentence hanging in the air as though the result is too terrible to describe. What if man should do this?

Then God's loving solution follows. He says, "drive him out, cast him out of the garden, and put at the gate of Eden the cherubim" [throughout the rest of Scripture cherubim appear; these are what we might call angelic animals, related to the holiness of God], and a flaming sword which turns every way—but now, notice, "to guard the way *to* the tree of life." It does not say, "to keep men from coming to the tree of life." That is not what the barrier is for. It is to guard the way *to* the tree of life, so that men come the right way and not the wrong.

So, although this passage is usually read as though God has barred man from the tree of life, and there is no way to get back in, that is not true. There is a way in, but it is no longer a physical way. That is what this text is telling us. Man must be kept from trying to come through some physical means, but must be forced to find the right way back. That is what the cherubim and the flaming sword are for. They absolutely cut off any other way to God than the right way. There is no other way, only one.

This is why what you do with your body, religiously, is of no importance whatever unless it is a genuine reflection of what you do with your spirit, religiously. This explains why you can come to church every Sunday morning, sit in the pews, nod your head, pray, stand, sit down again, genuflect—anything you want; but if the heart is not doing the same thing it is an ugly, distasteful thing in God's sight, and he has no regard for it at all. There is no way to come to God by *doing* something; none at all. The physical approach to God is completely cut off.

The Tree Is for Healing

But now read the words of the Lord Jesus in the Gospel of John:

> I am the way, and the truth, and the life; no one comes to the Father, but by me (John 14:6).

That is the only way there is. It is the way to begin the Christian life, but it is also the way to continue the

Christian life. Do you know the way to the tree of life? In the Book of Revelation we read that the tree of life is for healing (Rev. 22:2). Do you know how to find healing, do you know the way to the place of healing? When your spirit has been torn and broken, or you are pressed by despair, or wounded by sorrow or grief, heartache or guilt, whatever it may be, do you know the way to the place of healing, to the place where the living waters flow? Have you learned not to go only once, but many, many times; to drink again and again of the water of life? Do you know what that means?

Do you know what Jesus meant when he said to the woman at the well, "I will put in you a well of living water, so that you do not need to come to this well for satisfaction. You will find it within you, and you can drink any time you want to" (John 4:14). Have you learned to drink of this well within when the pressure is on you; to retreat from outward circumstances for the moment and come again to that living fountain of water, springing up within you? To take by quiet faith his promised supply, to partake of his patience and his power, and so to meet the circumstances with a mind at ease, relaxed, trusting, no longer fearful. Do you know what that means? That is the function of the tree of life.

This physical exclusion from Eden is why the body of man must die. The Apostle Paul tells us that is so even for Christians. He says, "we know that our old self was crucified with him so *that the sinful body might be destroyed*" (Rom. 6:6), but that we might live with him in the realm of the spirit and soul. This is why our bodies are dying and we cannot come to God, physically. We cannot find our way visibly into his presence.

We cannot until the problem of the body is resolved in resurrection. But the glorious truth is, as Hebrews declares to us, that the blood of Jesus Christ has opened for us a new and living way into the holy place (Heb. 10:19,20), and there again we live in the presence of the tree of life in the garden of Eden. Spiritually and psychologically (in the realm of emotions and mind) we are to live in the presence of God because a way has been opened back to the tree of life.

Let me summarize briefly the teaching of this passage. Look at the whole process. First, *temptation*. How familiar we are with that! That is followed immediately by *death*, which grips us and casts a gloom over our lives, bores us and frustrates us, and makes us feel despairing, discouraged, and defeated. Then we come to the place of *repentance*, where we admit the facts as God sees them. Then we experience the flowing of *grace*, the promise of victory and of restoration, accompanied by those helpful measures by which we are made to see our dependence upon him.

Next responds the spirit and in *faith*, we believe what God has said and are changed and strengthened. We are remade again, in what the New Testament calls "the renewing of the mind by the Holy Spirit." Then there is the public *acknowledgment* on God's part, clothing us with Christ's peace, Christ's righteousness, Christ's power and poise, so that we become panic-proof, no longer disturbed by the circumstances around. It ends by finding our way back to the place of the *healing* of our mind, heart and spirit—spiritual health!

Is that not also what the New Testament develops for us? Have you any questions left as to whether Genesis is from the hand and mind of God? The whole gospel of grace is given to us right at the beginning, so that we might live in this world, amidst all the problems of our daily experience.

Thank you, our Holy Father, for the way back that is open to all of us, the way to the One who himself is the tree of life—the way, the truth, and the life. We must live by him. We have no other place to live in these days. We pray that each of us, young and old alike, may grasp more firmly the vast importance of learning to live by the Lord Jesus, by a constant communication with his life, his grace, his strength, his power. Lord, open our eyes to understand these things so that we may be men and women who so conduct ourselves as to be mysteries, puzzles, to those around who cannot understand where we get this amazing strength, this unflappable poise, this startling ability to handle life at its worst, without failing. We ask it in Jesus' name. Amen.

DISCOVERY BIBLE STUDY BOOKS

OLD TESTAMENT STUDIES

Expository Studies in Genesis 2 and 3
(Understanding Man)
Ray C. Stedman

Expository Studies in Genesis 4-11
(The Beginnings)
Ray C. Stedman

Expository Studies in Esther
(The Queen and I)
Ray C. Stedman

Expository Studies in Jeremiah
(Death of a Nation)
Ray C. Stedman

The New Covenant in the Old Testament
David H. Roper

NEW TESTAMENT STUDIES

Expository Studies in Matthew 13
(Behind History)
Ray C. Stedman

Expository Studies in Mark 1-8
(The Servant Who Rules)
Ray C. Stedman

Expository Studies in Mark 8-16
(The Ruler Who Serves)
Ray C. Stedman

Jesus Teaches On Prayer
(Luke)
Ray C. Stedman

Secrets of the Spirit
(John 13-17)
Ray C. Stedman

Authentic Christianity
(II Corinthians)
Ray C. Stedman

Expository Studies in Romans 1-8
(From Guilt to Glory, Vol. I)
Ray C. Stedman

Expository Studies in Romans 9-16
(From Guilt to Glory, Vol. II)
Ray C. Stedman

Expository Studies in Ephesians 1-3
(Riches in Christ)
Ray C. Stedman

Body Life
(Ephesians 4)
Ray C. Stedman

Expository Studies in Ephesians 6
(Spiritual Warfare)
Ray C. Stedman

The Law That Sets You Free
(James)
David H. Roper

OTHER DISCOVERY BIBLE STUDY BOOKS

Basics of Bible Interpretation
Bob W. Smith

Family Life: God's View of Relationships
Ray C. Stedman with David H. Roper, Jack Crabtree,
Jean McAllister, John Fischer, Del Fuller

When All Else Fails . . . Read The Directions
Bob W. Smith

Dying To Live
Bob W. Smith

Love Story . . . The Real Thing
Bob W. Smith